INSIDE THE Windows NT File System

Microsoft
PRESS

Helen Custer

AUTHOR OF *INSIDE WINDOWS NT*

PUBLISHED BY
Microsoft Press
A Division of Microsoft Corporation
One Microsoft Way
Redmond, Washington 98052-6399

Library of Congress Cataloging-in-Publication Data
Custer, Helen, 1961-
    Inside the Windows NT file system / Helen Custer.
        p.   cm.
    Includes bibliographical references and index.
    ISBN 1-55615-660-X
    1. Operating systems (Computers)   2. Windows NT.   I. Title.
QA76.76.O63C892   1994
005.4'469--dc20   94-15139
                                                CIP

Printed and bound in the United States of America.

    5 6 7 8 9   MLML 9 8 7 6

Distributed to the book trade in Canada by Macmillan of Canada, a division of Canada
Publishing Corporation.

A CIP catalogue record for this book is available from the British Library.

Microsoft Press books are available through booksellers and distributors worldwide. For further
information about international editions, contact your local Microsoft Corporation office. Or
contact Microsoft Press International directly at fax (206) 936-7329.

Acquisitions Editor: Dean Holmes
Project Editor: Maureen Williams Zimmerman
Manuscript Editor: Erin O'Connor
Technical Editor: Wm. Jeff Carey

Dedicated to little Kathy
and Grandpa Joe

CONTENTS

PREFACE

The NT file system (NTFS) is one of several interesting Windows NT components I didn't have time to cover in my earlier book, *Inside Windows NT*. I wrote this book documenting NTFS because reliable disk storage is such a critical part of an advanced operating system. I assume throughout this book that the reader has a basic understanding of the Windows NT architecture and of simple disk caching and virtual memory principles.

It was a pleasure to work with the file system team on this project. Special thanks go to Tom Miller for generously sharing his expertise, his notes, and his time, and to Gary Kimura for presenting alternative viewpoints on the file system design and for providing technical reviews. Thanks also to Bob Rinne, Brian Andrew, Peter Galvin, Mike Glass, David Goebel, Norbert Kusters, Matthew Bradburn, and Bill McJohn. And thanks once again to Dave Cutler, Lou Perazzoli, and Ron Burk for supporting my work, and to the talented staff at Microsoft Press for their exceptional editing and production support.

Finally, many thanks to my lifting partners during the past year, especially to Michael, Jill, Marsha, and Trish. You've taught me the sanity to be found in raw physical exertion. (Never mind the torn shoulder and broken toes.)

Helen Custer
April, 1994

INTRODUCTION

The *NT File System* (NTFS) was created specifically for use with the Windows NT operating system. NTFS is a new file system with advanced capabilities that make it appropriate for the Windows NT high-end operating system environment. Tom Miller, the architect of NTFS,[1] has an extensive background in transaction processing and recoverable database systems, and his expertise in those areas is manifest in the design and features of NTFS.

NTFS was written concurrently with Windows NT. Approximately two years into the Windows NT project, the engineers started to run the emerging operating system and to use it as their development environment. A year later, NTFS was stable enough to use and the developers were encouraged to convert their hard disks from the file allocation table (FAT) file system to NTFS. Tom Miller describes this period with some discomfiture:

> Working on file systems is probably the worst place to be [in operating systems development]. If your system bug-checks or something funny happens to your display, you can usually reboot the system and continue working. But if something goes wrong with your disk, you often can't work at all. People get very irate when there are file system bugs. Nobody wants their permanent storage to become impermanent.

When an operating system under construction is also being used as the development platform, dealing with software bugs is an everyday adventure. Though inconvenient and often frustrating for developers, using the system in this way ensures that bugs will be found and fixed quickly and guarantees that more bugs will be discovered than the testing process alone would uncover. But customers should never experience an unstable system, especially an unstable file system. Their permanent disk storage should remain permanent. Losing all or part of a hard disk is one of the most traumatic kinds of system failure an end user can experience.

It was concern for the customer's disk storage that drove the design of NTFS. Tom and the NTFS team broke new ground in building a file system that not only is more reliable and secure than existing file systems but has an

---

1. Other major contributors include Gary Kimura, Brian Andrew, and David Goebel.

important additional feature: it is *recoverable*. When an operating system or hardware failure occurs, NTFS has the ability to reconstruct itself so that the volume (partition) remains accessible and consistent and the directory structure is not corrupted.

NTFS is appropriate for all types of users but should be especially appealing to users who have relied primarily on minicomputer and mainframe operating systems in the past—systems whose designers gave careful consideration to the reliability and security of data storage. With its recovery capabilities, NTFS sets a new standard of reliability for file systems.

The purpose of this book is to document the design of NTFS. However, some justification for the creation of NTFS seems in order, both because writing a file system is a long, arduous task and because NTFS introduces a new file storage format. Chapter One addresses why the development team decided to create NTFS in spite of the challenge.

Chapter Two describes the theoretical models underlying the NTFS design, and Chapter Three details the file system's internal structure. Chapter Four introduces file system recoverability and explains how NTFS recovers a volume after a system failure occurs. Another new feature, hard disk fault-tolerance, is available for use with all Windows NT file systems. It is especially valuable when used with NTFS because it builds on NTFS recoverability to produce particularly robust disk storage. Fault tolerance is described in Chapter Five. Chapter Six documents NTFS data compression, a built-in feature of NTFS that is new in Windows NT version 3.5. Chapter Seven discusses short file name generation, an NTFS capability that allows MS-DOS clients to access files with long names.

WHY CREATE ANOTHER FILE SYSTEM?

In 1988, Microsoft already supported two file systems—the FAT file system for MS-DOS and Microsoft Windows and the high-performance file system (HPFS) for OS/2—so naturally, Tom Miller and the other developers responsible for Windows NT file systems thought a lot about whether NT needed a new file system at all. Unfortunately, the FAT file system and HPFS suffered from limitations that made them either less reliable than a file system for Windows NT should be or unable to handle the large system configurations that were expected to run the Windows NT operating system. After careful consideration, the team decided to create a new file system, but NTFS is nevertheless heavily influenced by the implementations of the FAT file system and HPFS, as well as by certain features required by the POSIX standard.[1]

The first section of this chapter describes the requirements of high-end client-server and business applications for a Windows NT file system. The second section examines the advanced features NTFS implements for those applications.

1.1 High-End File System Requirements

MS-DOS uses the FAT file system, which was originally designed for floppy disks of a relatively small size, generally 1 MB or smaller. As hard disks became the standard storage device for personal computers and over time grew larger, they began to stretch the limits of the FAT file system. The OS/2

---

1. A collection of international standards for UNIX-style operating system interfaces, ISO/IEC 9945-1 (IEEE Standard 1003.1-1990).

operating system introduced HPFS to address some of the limitations of the FAT file system. HPFS, for example, greatly improved file access times for large directories and could be used on hard disks up to 4 GB (gigabyte—a billion bytes) in size.[2]

The FAT file system worked well for small disks, and HPFS added some new capabilities, greater file access efficiency, and support for larger media. However, neither file system was entirely suitable for Windows NT, an operating system designed for sophisticated, "mission-critical" applications:

- Client-server applications such as file servers, compute servers, and database servers

- High-powered engineering and scientific applications

- Network applications for large corporate systems

For such applications, a highly reliable and secure file system is a requirement. Compromising the important data in an airline scheduling system or a bank database server, for instance, could wreak great havoc.

Corporate file system requirements include data recovery capabilities, data security, fault tolerance, and support for even larger storage media than HPFS provides.

1.1.1 Recoverability

As far as disk I/O is concerned, personal computer users have tended to care most about speed—they've just wanted to get their work done fast. As Windows NT moves the personal computer into more businesses and corporations, however, the reliability of the data stored on the system becomes increasingly important relative to the speed with which a user can access data on a disk drive. In other words, if the system fails and a disk drive is corrupted or becomes inaccessible, the speed of the preceding I/O operations is largely irrelevant.

To address the requirement for reliable data storage and data access reliability, the team designed NTFS as a recoverable file system based on a transaction-processing model. In the event of a power failure or other system failure, NTFS reconstructs disk volumes and returns them to a consistent state. An NTFS recovery operation occurs automatically the first time the disk is accessed after a failure and takes only a few seconds to be com-

---

2. The disk size HPFS could support was expanded later to 2 TB (terabyte—a trillion bytes).

pleted, regardless of the size of the disk. In addition, NTFS uses redundant storage for its vital sectors, so that if one location on the disk goes bad, NTFS can still access the volume's critical file system data. This redundancy of file system data is in contrast to the on-disk structures of both the MS-DOS FAT file system and the OS/2 HPFS, which have single sectors containing critical file system data. If a read error occurs in one of these sectors, an entire volume is lost.[3]

1.1.2 Security

Data security is of primary importance to businesses and government agencies that process private or sensitive information—banks, hospitals, and national defense–related agencies, for example. Such customers need guarantees that their data will be secure from unauthorized access.

Security in NTFS is derived directly from the Windows NT object model. An open file is implemented as a file object with a security descriptor stored on disk as a part of the file.[4] Before a process can open a handle to any object, including a file object, the Windows NT security system verifies that the process has appropriate authorization to do so. The security descriptor, combined with the requirement that a user log on to the system and provide a password to identify himself, ensures that no process can access a file unless given specific permission to do so by a system administrator or by the file's owner.

1.1.3 Data Redundancy and Fault Tolerance

In addition to recoverability of file system data, some customers require that their own data not be endangered by a power outage or catastrophic system failure. The NTFS recovery capabilities do ensure that the file system on a volume remains accessible, but they make no guarantees for complete recovery of user files. For banking or other applications that can't risk losing file data, data redundancy provides an extra level of protection.

The Windows NT layered driver model enables NTFS to communicate with a fault tolerant disk driver, which in turn communicates with a hard disk

---

3. The Windows NT implementations of the FAT file system and HPFS are improvements over the original implementations because they use the Windows NT fault tolerant driver to increase their reliability. See Chapter Five, "Volume Management and Fault Tolerance," for more information on FtDisk, the Windows NT fault tolerant driver.

4. For more information about security descriptors and file objects, see *Inside Windows NT*, Chapter 3, "The Object Manager and Object Security," and Chapter 8, "The I/O System."

driver to write data to disk. This allows a Windows NT system to establish fault tolerant disk storage by installing an additional driver.[5] The fault tolerant driver can *mirror,* or duplicate, data from one disk on another disk so that a redundant copy can always be retrieved. The fault tolerant driver also allows data to be written in *stripes* across three or more disks, using the equivalent of one disk to maintain parity information. If the data on one disk is lost or becomes inaccessible, the driver can reconstruct the disk's contents by means of exclusive-OR operations.[6]

1.1.4 Large Disks and Large Files

Engineering and other scientific applications often store and process extremely large quantities of information. Hard disks with over 2 GB of storage and disk arrays with 8 or 10 GB of storage are no longer uncommon. NTFS supports very large disks and large files more efficiently than either the FAT file system or HPFS.

The FAT file system uses a table 16 bits wide to record the allocation status of a disk volume. Because a volume is divided into same-size allocation units—called *clusters*—and each cluster must be uniquely numbered using 16 bits, the FAT can support a maximum of 2^{16}, or 65,536, clusters per volume (although the FAT reserves some of this space for itself). The cluster size can be increased or decreased depending on the size of the volume. However, volumes beyond a certain size require very large cluster sizes, which results in wasted disk space—a problem known as *internal fragmentation*. A cluster size of 1 KB, for example, covers a 65-MB disk, but a cluster size of at least 10 KB would be required to cover a 640-MB disk. Given that the cluster size must be a power of 2, a 16-KB cluster size is actually used for a 640-MB disk; that is, allocations are made in 16-KB increments. If a file is 512 bytes or 17 KB, for example, only a fraction of the allocated space is used to store data. In any case, a single FAT volume is limited to containing 65,518 files (the maximum number of available clusters), regardless of the size of the disk.

HPFS uses 32 bits to enumerate its allocation units, a strategy that yields 2^{32}, or over 4 billion, numbers. HPFS uses signed numbers, however,

---

5. Fault tolerant disk support is available only in the Windows NT Advanced Server product.

6. The mirroring capability of the fault tolerant driver corresponds to the redundant array of inexpensive disks (RAID) level 1 definition, and the striping capability corresponds to the RAID level 5 definition. See Patterson et al. in the bibliography at the end of this book.

which reduces this number to 2 billion possible allocation units on an HPFS volume. Rather than clusters, HPFS allocates disk space in terms of physical sectors, each set at 512 bytes. This lack of flexibility can be a problem, particularly in Asian markets, where disk drives commonly have a hardware sector size of 1024 bytes. HPFS can't be used on such drives because disks can't allocate space in increments smaller than their hardware sector size. HPFS is also limited to a maximum file size of 4 GB.

NTFS allocates clusters and uses 64 bits to number them, which results in a possible 2^{64} (over 16,000,000,000,000,000,000, or 16 billion billion) clusters, each up to 4 KB. Each file can be of virtually infinite size, that is, 2^{64} bytes long. As in the FAT file system, the cluster size in NTFS is adjustable, but it is not required to grow proportionally to the disk size. NTFS uses a cluster size of 512 bytes on small disks and a maximum cluster size of 4 KB on large disks. Although NTFS uses a 64-bit (8-byte) disk address to represent each *run* (disk allocation), it "encodes" the addresses so that they occupy only 3 to 5 bytes per run. (Look ahead to Figure 3-12 in Chapter Three to see an example of address encoding.) HPFS uses 12 bytes to represent each run.

1.2 New Features in NTFS

In addition to making NTFS a recoverable, secure, reliable, and efficient file system for client-server and other high-end systems, its designers added new features to the file system that will allow it to support the broadest range of both existing and future personal computer applications.

1.2.1 Multiple Data Streams

In NTFS, each unit of information associated with a file, including its name, its owner, its time stamps, its contents, and so on, is implemented as a file attribute (object attribute). Each attribute consists of a single *stream*, that is, a simple sequence of bytes. This generic implementation makes it easy to add more attributes (and therefore more streams) to a file. Because a file's data is "just another attribute" of the file and new attributes can be added, NTFS files (and file directories) can contain multiple data streams.

An NTFS file has one default data stream, which has no name. An application can create additional, named, data streams and access them by referring to their names. To avoid altering the Win32 I/O *application programming interfaces* (APIs), which take a string as a file name argument, the NTFS team used a syntax trick to provide applications with access to multiple data streams in a file. Because the colon (:) is a reserved character, it can serve as a separator between the file name and the data stream name, as illustrated in this example:

```
myfile.dat:stream2
```

Each stream has a separate allocation size (how much disk space has been reserved for it), an actual size (how many bytes the caller has used), and a valid data length (how much of the stream has been initialized). In addition, each stream is given a separate file lock used to lock byte ranges and allow concurrent access. In order to reduce processing overhead, sharing is done per file, rather than per stream.

One way in which NTFS uses multiple data streams is to store data originating from Apple Macintosh systems. Macintosh systems use two streams per file, one to store data and the other to store resource information, such as the file type and the icon used to represent the file. Because NTFS allows multiple data streams, a Macintosh user can copy an entire Macintosh folder (analogous to a directory) to a Windows NT server, and another Macintosh user can copy the folder from the server without losing resource information. Other applications could use the multiple data stream feature as well. A backup utility, for example, might use an extra data stream to store backup-specific time stamps on files. Or an archival utility might implement hierarchical storage in which files that are older than a certain date or that haven't been accessed for a specified period of time are moved to tape. The utility could copy the file to tape, set the file's default data stream to 0, and add a data stream that specifies the name and location of the tape on which the file is stored.

1.2.2 Unicode-Based Names

Like Windows NT as a whole, NTFS is fully Unicode enabled, using Unicode characters to store names of files, directories, and volumes. Unicode, a 16-bit character-coding scheme, allows each character in each of the world's languages to be uniquely represented, which aids in moving data easily from one country to another. Unicode is an improvement over the FAT and HPFS representation of international characters; they use a double-byte coding scheme that stores some characters in 8 bits and others in 16 bits, a technique that requires loading various code pages to establish the available characters. Unicode has a unique representation for each character and therefore doesn't depend on which code page is loaded. Each directory and file name in a path name can be as many as 255 characters long and can contain Unicode characters, embedded spaces, and multiple periods.

1.2.3 General Indexing Facility

The NTFS architecture is structured to allow indexing of file attributes on a disk volume, which enables the file system to efficiently locate files that match certain criteria—for example, all the files in a particular directory. The FAT file system indexes file names but doesn't sort them, making lookups in large directories slow. HPFS indexes and sorts file names as NTFS does, but the design of NTFS allows for indexing other file attributes as well. If a file's author were an important indexing key, for example, NTFS could be easily altered to efficiently locate all files with a specific author.[7]

1.2.4 Bad-Cluster Remapping

Ordinarily, if a program tries to read data from a bad disk sector, the read operation fails and the data in the allocated cluster becomes inaccessible. However, if the disk is formatted as a fault tolerant NTFS volume, the Windows NT fault tolerant driver dynamically retrieves a good copy of the data that was stored on the bad sector and then sends NTFS a warning that the sector is bad. NTFS allocates a new cluster, replacing the cluster in which the bad sector resides, and copies the data to the new cluster. It flags the bad cluster and no longer uses it. This data recovery and dynamic cluster remapping is an especially useful feature for file servers and fault tolerant systems or for any application that can't afford to lose data. If the fault tolerant driver isn't loaded when a sector goes bad, NTFS still replaces the cluster and doesn't reuse it, but it can't recover the data that was on the bad sector.

1.2.5 POSIX Support

Windows NT contains a POSIX subsystem that runs POSIX applications and shells. With this capability comes the need for the file system to deal appropriately with POSIX files. In particular, the POSIX standard requires the file system to support case-sensitive file and directory names, a "file-change-time" time stamp (which is different from the MS-DOS "time-last-modified" stamp), and hard links. NTFS implements each of these features. NTFS does not implement POSIX symbolic links in its first release, but it can be extended to do so.

---

7. In the current release of NTFS, only the file name attribute is indexed.

1.2.6 Removable Disks

NTFS is designed for use on both fixed and removable disks. Because the FAT file system is a de facto standard for floppy disks, Microsoft has no plans to support NTFS on floppy disks. However, NTFS can be used on other types of removable media, such as Bernoulli disks. Windows NT is a secure operating system, and NTFS extends that security to files; therefore, removable disks formatted for NTFS are protected by the same security mechanisms as those used for fixed disks.

CHAPTER TWO

THE NTFS MODEL

Despite the new requirements for recoverability and security in NTFS and the many new features its designers incorporated into it, the first and foremost requirement was that NTFS be a reliable and fast file system. It had to handle standard file system operations, such as booting the system and loading executable images, and it had to plug into the loadable, layered Windows NT driver model established by the I/O system. It had to do these things while achieving performance that would meet or exceed that of existing personal computer file systems. NTFS uses several models to achieve these goals:

- From the Windows NT I/O system's point of view, NTFS is just another driver loaded into the operating system and available for processing I/O requests. NTFS can be layered on top of or beneath other drivers in the I/O system's layered driver model.

- From another vantage point, NTFS is a sophisticated relational database that incorporates the latest technical advances in data logging and recovery as well as new features such as multiple data streams and indexing of file attributes.

- From yet another point of view, NTFS participates in the Windows NT object model, operating on file objects whose security is ensured by the Windows NT object manager and security system.

2.1 The Layered Driver Model

In Windows NT, NTFS and other file systems are loadable drivers. They can be added to or removed from the operating system as they're needed. All drivers work within the context of the Windows NT I/O system and are invoked indirectly by applications that use Win32 or other I/O APIs. As Figure 2-1 shows, the Windows NT environment subsystems call NT system services, which in turn locate the appropriate loaded drivers and call them.

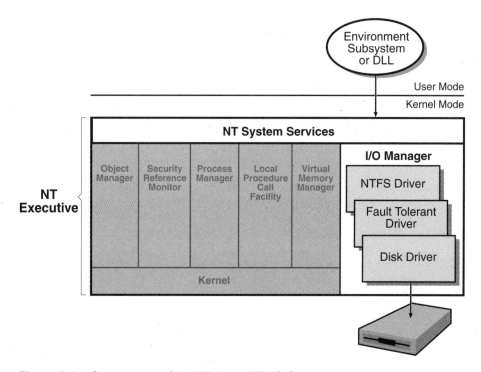

Figure 2-1. Components of the Windows NT I/O System

The layered drivers pass I/O requests to each other by calling the NT executive's I/O manager. Relying on the I/O manager as an intermediary allows each driver to maintain independence so that it can be loaded or unloaded without affecting other drivers. In addition, the NTFS driver interacts with three other NT executive components, shown in the left side of Figure 2-2, that are closely related to file systems.

The *log file service* (LFS), developed by Brian Andrew, is a module of the Windows NT executive that provides services for maintaining a log of disk writes. The *log file* it writes is used to recover an NTFS-formatted volume in the case of a system failure.

The *cache manager* is a component of the Windows NT executive written by Tom Miller that provides system-wide caching services for NTFS and other file system drivers, including network file system drivers (servers and redirectors). All file systems implemented for Windows NT access cached

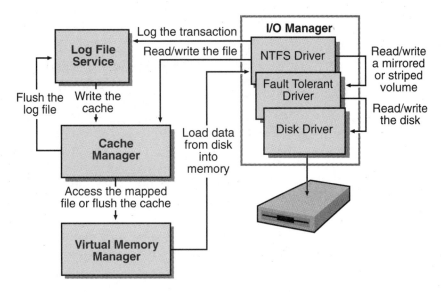

Figure 2-2. NTFS and Related NT Executive Components

files by mapping them into virtual memory[1] and reading and writing to virtual memory. The cache manager provides a specialized file system interface to the Windows NT virtual memory manager (VM manager) for this purpose. When a program tries to access a part of a file that is not loaded into the cache (a *cache miss*), the VM manager calls NTFS to access the disk driver and obtain the file contents from disk. The cache manager optimizes disk I/O by using its *lazy writer,* a set of system threads that calls the VM manager to flush cache contents to disk as a background activity (asynchronous disk writing).

The relationships shown for NTFS in Figure 2-2 are the same as those for the other Windows NT–supported file systems: the FAT file system, HPFS, and network file systems. The only difference is that these file systems don't call the log file service to log transactions.

2.2 Relational Database and Transaction-Processing Models

The usefulness of database software lies in its ability to extract information based on any number of criteria or combinations of criteria. The most

---

1. See *Inside Windows NT,* Chapter 6, "The Virtual Memory Manager," for a discussion of virtual memory in Windows NT.

powerful database packages can handle complicated queries and perform database updates with great speed.

A file system can be viewed as a type of database that applications and utilities query for information about files. For example, the Dir command on MS-DOS systems and the *ls* command on POSIX systems call their respective file systems to obtain a list of the names of files and subdirectories in a directory. Typically, a file system "query" requests a collection of file names that fit a particular criterion. By structuring NTFS as a database, its designers could exploit the benefits of a database design, such as the ability to easily select a collection of files based on some attribute or the ability to store such collections in sorted indexes for fast retrieval.

Another aspect of the NTFS design, one closely related to the database theme, is the NTFS use of a transaction-processing model in recording changes to a volume. Transaction processing is a technique for handling modifications to a database so that system failures don't affect the correctness or integrity of the database. The basic tenet of transaction processing is that there are some database operations, called *transactions,* which are "all-or-nothing" propositions. The separate disk updates that make up the transaction must be executed *atomically;* that is, once the transaction begins to execute, all of its disk updates must be completed. If a system failure interrupts the transaction, the part that has been completed must be undone, or *rolled back.* The rollback operation returns the database to a previously known and consistent state, as if the transaction had never existed.

Suppose that a bank customer is transferring $300 from a savings account to a checking account using an automatic teller machine. She enters the transfer operation, and database software begins to process the request by subtracting $300 from the customer's savings account. Now suppose that the power fails and the system crashes. If transaction-processing principles were not in effect and the computer came back online with the database as it was when the power failed, the bank's records would show $300 less in the customer's savings account than she previously had, with nothing added to her checking account. Clearly, failures of this kind are unacceptable in financial software.

By specifying a funds transfer operation as an atomic transaction, the transaction-processing software ensures that the entire set of sub-operations—withdrawing from savings and depositing into checking—is treated as a single operation. If the system fails in the middle of this transaction, transaction-processing software, which has kept a record of the transactions in progress and how far they have gotten, can undo the half-completed transfer of funds by crediting the customer's savings account when the system comes back online.

NTFS uses the transaction-processing model to implement its file system recovery feature. If a program initiates an I/O operation that alters the structure of the NTFS file system—changes the directory structure, extends a file, allocates space for a new file, and so on—NTFS treats that operation as an atomic transaction. It guarantees that the transaction is either completed or, if the system fails while executing the transaction, rolled back. Suppose, for example, that a user creates a file and NTFS inserts the new file name into its directory structure just before the system goes down. The directory entry exists, but the disk space for the file has not yet been allocated. Treating file creation as an atomic operation ensures that NTFS (that is, the "database") maintains internal consistency. In the example, NTFS will roll back the file creation operation, removing the file name from its directory structure.

NTFS keeps track of the contents of a volume in a relational database, a table containing rows of records and columns of attributes. The rows of the *master file table* (MFT), as the database is called, correspond to individual files on the disk, and the columns correspond to file attributes. A directory is viewed as a file, with a slightly different set of attributes. Figure 2-3 depicts the logical structure of the MFT and the various attributes that can exist in a file or a directory.

Instead of viewing a file as just a repository for textual or binary data, the NTFS model views a file as a collection of attributes, one of which is the

	Standard Information	File Name	Security Descriptor	Data	HPFS Extended Attributes (EAs)
File 0				unnamed stream	
1				unnamed stream	
2				unnamed stream	
5 (directory)				Index Root / Index Allocation / Bitmap	

Figure 2-3. File and Directory Records in the Master File Table

data it contains. A relational database structure allows the file system to be easily extended. If a user creates a file, NTFS simply fills in a new row in the table. If a program adds an attribute[2] or a second data stream, or if a file is given an alternate MS-DOS name (see Chapter Seven), NTFS inserts another column in the MFT for the affected file, as Figure 2-4 shows.

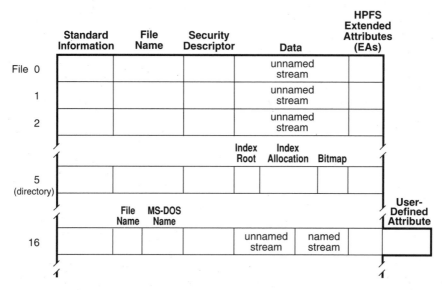

Figure 2-4. Adding Attributes and a Data Stream to an MFT Record

Like many relational databases, NTFS can create indexes for attributes. In a file system, an *index* is a collection of files selected for some attribute. A directory in NTFS, for instance, is an index of file names with a particular path prefixed to them. Internally, NTFS can create an index based on any attribute that is specified as index-able, but currently only file names are indexed. NTFS sorts its file name indexes by means of an efficient data structure called a *b+ tree*, in which file names are collated lexicographically, allowing for quick lookup of queries such as *dir str*.**.

Although NTFS uses the relational database model for parts of its implementation, it departs from the model when the model doesn't suit the purposes of a file system. For example, NTFS must implement a hierarchical directory structure like that used by the FAT file system and HPFS. By adding

---

2. User-defined attributes are not currently supported in Windows NT. However, the architecture allows for the enabling of user-defined attributes in the future.

directories to the MFT and treating them as files, NTFS creates a hierarchical structure within the traditional relational database table structure. As Figures 2-3 and 2-4 showed, in place of the data attribute, a directory record contains three attributes used to implement the directory's file name index.

2.3 The Object Model

NTFS participates in the Windows NT object model by implementing files as objects. This allows files to be shared and protected by the object manager, the component of Windows NT that manages all executive-level objects.

An application creates or accesses a file just as it does other NT objects: by means of object handles. By the time an I/O request reaches NTFS, the Windows NT object manager and security system have already verified that the calling process has the authority to access the file object in the way it is attempting to. The security system has compared the caller's security token to the entries in the access control list for the file object. (See *Inside Windows NT,* Chapter 3, for more information about access control lists.) The I/O manager has also transformed the file handle into a pointer to a file object. NTFS uses the information in the file object to access the file on disk.

Figure 2-5 on the next page shows the data structures that link the memory-based object architecture to the file system's on-disk structure.

NTFS is called with a pointer to a file object. It follows several pointers to get from the file object to the location of the file on disk. As Figure 2-5 shows, a file object, which represents a single call to the open-file system service, points to a *stream control block* (SCB) for the file attribute that the caller is trying to read or write. In Figure 2-5, a process has opened both the data attribute and a user-defined attribute for the file. The SCBs represent individual file attributes and contain information about how to find specific attributes within a file. All the SCBs for a file point to a common data structure called a *file control block* (FCB). The FCB contains a pointer (actually, a file reference) to the file's record in the disk-based MFT.

As mentioned in Section 2.2, NTFS views a file as a collection of attributes, just as the Windows NT object manager views an object as a collection of attributes. NTFS uses the same read routine regardless of whether it is reading a file's data attribute, its security descriptor attribute, its file name attribute, or any of the file's other attributes. Similarly, when writing to a file, NTFS takes an attribute as a parameter and writes to that attribute. Because these object routines are generic, they can easily accommodate new attributes that may be added in the future.

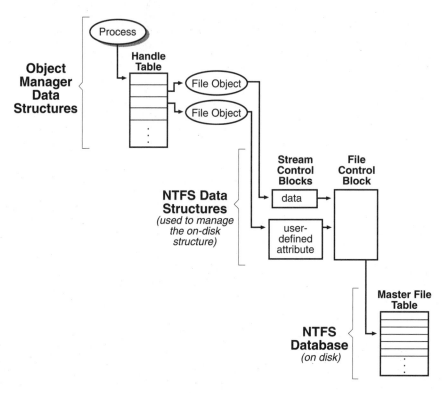

Figure 2-5. Locating an NTFS File

CHAPTER THREE

FILE SYSTEM STRUCTURE

Chapter Two described the software models the file system team borrowed from as they designed NTFS. This chapter sets the models aside and delves deeper into the NTFS implementation, looking especially at the on-disk structure and at some of the data structures NTFS uses to maintain the disk structure. It begins with an overview of NTFS concepts and terminology and follows that with a look at the important NTFS data structures. How NTFS stores data, including file name indexes, on disk is described next. The last section examines the files NTFS uses to manage the disk and to implement recovery.

3.1 NTFS Concepts and Terms

The structure of NTFS begins with a *volume.* A volume corresponds to a logical partition on a disk, and it is created when you format a disk or part of a disk for NTFS. You can also create a fault tolerant volume spanning multiple disks by using the Windows NT Disk Administrator utility.

A disk can have one volume or several. NTFS handles each volume independently of the others. Sample disk configurations for a 150-MB hard disk are illustrated in Figure 3-1 on the next page.

A volume consists of a series of files plus any additional unallocated space remaining on the disk partition. In the FAT file system and HPFS, a volume also contains areas specially formatted for use by the file system. An NTFS volume, however, stores all file system data, such as bitmaps and directories, and even the system bootstrap, as ordinary files.

NTFS is like the FAT file system in that it uses the cluster as its fundamental unit of disk allocation. The cluster size on a volume, or *cluster factor,* is established by the NTFS Format utility when a user formats the volume. The

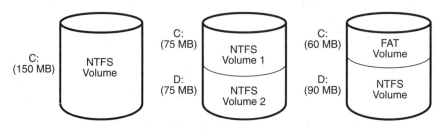

Figure 3-1. Sample Disk Configurations

cluster factor varies with the size of the volume, but it is an integral number of physical sectors, always a power of 2 (1 sector, 2 sectors, 4 sectors, 8 sectors, and so on), as shown in Figure 3-2. The cluster factor is expressed as the number of bytes in the cluster, such as 512 bytes, 1 KB, or 2 KB.

Internally, NTFS refers only to clusters and is unaware of a disk's sector size. Unlike HPFS, which mandates a 512-byte physical sector as its unit of allocation, NTFS uses the cluster as its unit of allocation in order to maintain its independence from physical sector sizes. This allows NTFS to efficiently support very large disks by using a larger cluster size or to support nonstandard disks that have something other than a 512-byte sector size. On a 600-MB or larger volume, for example, use of a cluster size greater than 512 bytes can reduce fragmentation and speed allocation, at a small cost in terms of wasted disk space. The NTFS Format utility automatically determines an appropriate cluster size, but the system administrator can modify that value.[1]

NTFS refers to physical locations on a disk by means of *logical cluster numbers* (LCNs). LCNs are simply the numbering of all clusters from the beginning of the volume to the end. To convert an LCN to a physical disk address, NTFS multiplies the LCN by the cluster factor to get the physical byte offset on the volume, as the disk driver interface requires.

As described in Section 2.2, NTFS maintains a file called the master file table (MFT), which is the heart of the NTFS volume structure. Logically, the MFT contains one row for each file on the volume, including a row for the

---

1. The Format utility uses a cluster size of 512 bytes (or the hardware sector size if it is larger than 512 bytes) for disks up to 512 MB. For larger disks up to 1 GB, it uses a cluster size of 1 KB. For disks larger than 1 GB, up to 2 GB, it uses a cluster size of 2 KB. For disks larger than 2 GB, it uses a cluster size of 4 KB. This formula balances the inherent trade-off between the disk fragmentation that can occur with too small a cluster size and the wasted space (internal fragmentation) that can occur with too large a cluster size.

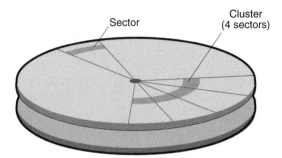

Figure 3-2. Sectors and a Cluster on a Disk

MFT itself. In addition to the MFT, each NTFS volume contains a boot file (described later) and a set of files containing data called *metadata* that is used to implement the file system structure. The rest of the files on an NTFS volume are normal user files and directories, as shown in Figure 3-3.

The MFT is implemented as an array of file records. An MFT "row," representing one file on the disk, usually consists of one file record. However, if a file has a large number of attributes or becomes highly fragmented, more than one file record might be needed. In such a case, the first record, which stores the locations of the others, is called the *base file record.*

A file on an NTFS volume is identified by a 64-bit value called a *file reference.* The file reference consists of a file number and a sequence number. The file number corresponds to the position of the file's file record in the MFT minus one (or to the position of the base file record minus one if the file has more than one file record). The file reference sequence number,

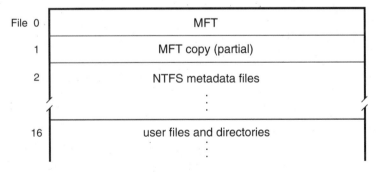

Figure 3-3. NTFS Metadata and User File Records in the MFT

which is incremented each time an MFT file record position is reused, enables NTFS to perform internal consistency checks. A file reference is illustrated in Figure 3-4.

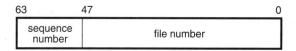

Figure 3-4. File Reference

A file in NTFS was defined earlier as a set of attributes, including a file name attribute, a security descriptor attribute, and a data attribute. NTFS identifies an attribute by its name in uppercase letters preceded by a dollar sign ($), as in *$FILENAME* or *$DATA*. These attribute names, however, actually correspond to numeric type codes, which NTFS uses to order the attributes within a file record. Figure 3-5 illustrates an MFT record for a small file.

Each file attribute is stored as a separate stream of bytes within a file. Strictly speaking, NTFS doesn't read and write files—it reads and writes attribute streams. NTFS supplies these attribute operations: create, delete, read (byte range), and write (byte range). The read and write services normally operate on the file's unnamed data attribute. However, a caller can specify a different data attribute by using the named data stream syntax. (Refer to Figure 2-4 back on page 16.)

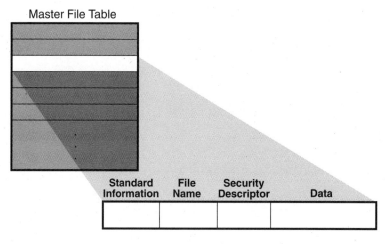

Figure 3-5. MFT Record for a Small File

The NTFS volume structure defines a set of standard attributes for files. These system-defined attributes have fixed attribute names and type codes, and NTFS determines the formats of their values. The attributes are listed in Figure 3-6 in the order in which they appear in a file record, although not all attributes are present for every file.

System-Defined Attribute	Description
Standard information	The file's "MS-DOS" attributes (read-only, read/write, and so on); its time stamps, including when the file was created or last modified; and how many directories point to the file (its *hard link count*).
Attribute list	A list of the attributes that make up the file and the file reference of the MFT file record in which each attribute is located. This seldom-used attribute is present when a file requires more than one MFT file record.
File name	The file's name in Unicode characters. A file can have multiple file name attributes, as it does when a POSIX hard link to a file exists or when a file with a long name has an automatically generated "short name" for access by MS-DOS and 16-bit Microsoft Windows applications.
Security descriptor	The security data structure that protects the file from unauthorized access. The security descriptor attribute specifies who owns the file and who can access it.
Data	The contents of the file. In NTFS, a file has one default unnamed data attribute and can have additional named data attributes (that is, a file can have multiple data streams). A directory has no default data attribute but can have optional named data attributes.
Index root, index allocation, bitmap (directories only)	Three attributes used to implement file name indexes for large directories.
HPFS extended attributes, HPFS extended attribute information	Two attributes used to implement HPFS-style extended attributes (EAs) for the OS/2 subsystem and for OS/2 clients of Windows NT file servers.

Figure 3-6. Standard File and Directory Attributes

3.2 On-Disk Structure

As earlier figures have shown, the rows (file records) of the MFT represent the files on an NTFS volume, and the columns represent file attributes. All file information is stored in attributes, and thus the rows and columns of the MFT describe all the information stored on an NTFS volume. The size of MFT file records for a volume—a minimum of 1 KB and a maximum of 4 KB—is determined when the volume is formatted.

The file attributes in an MFT record are ordered by (numerically) ascending type codes, with some attribute types appearing more than once—if a file has multiple data attributes, for example, or multiple file names. Figure 3-5 back on page 22 shows the attributes that are required for a file: the standard information attribute, the file name attribute, the security descriptor attribute, and the data attribute. Other attributes can also appear in an MFT file record as they are needed for a particular file.

Each attribute in a file record has a name (optional) and a value. Names are used primarily with the data attribute, to identify a second or third data stream in the file. An attribute's value is the byte stream composing the attribute. For example, the value of the $FILENAME attribute is the file's name; the value of the $DATA attribute is whatever bytes the user stored in the file. If a file is small, all its attributes and the attributes' values (its data, for example) fit in the file record. When the value of an attribute is stored directly in the MFT, the attribute is called a *resident attribute*. (In Figure 3-5, all attributes are resident.)

Each attribute begins with a standard header containing information about the attribute, which NTFS uses to manage the attributes in a generic way. The header, which is always resident, records whether the attribute's value is resident or nonresident. For resident attributes, the header also contains the offset from the header to the attribute's value and the length of the attribute's value, as Figure 3-7 illustrates for the file name attribute.

When an attribute's value is stored directly in the MFT, the time it takes NTFS to access the value is greatly reduced. Instead of looking up a file in a table and then reading a succession of allocation units to find the file's data (as the FAT file system, for example, does), NTFS accesses the disk once and retrieves the data immediately.

The attributes for a small directory, as well as for a small file, can be resident in the MFT, as Figure 3-8 shows. For a small directory, the index root attribute contains an index of file references for the files and the subdirectories in the directory.

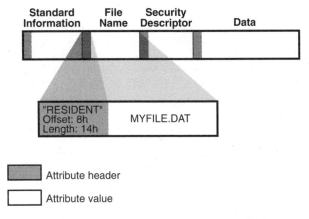

Figure 3-7. Resident Attribute Header and Value

Of course, many files and directories can't be squeezed into an MFT record, a 1-KB, 2-KB, or 4-KB data structure. If a particular attribute, such as a file's data attribute, is too large to be contained in the MFT file record, NTFS allocates a 2-KB area[2] on the disk, separate from the MFT. This area, called a *run* (or an *extent*), stores the value of the attribute (the file's data, for example). If the attribute's value later grows (if a user appends data to the file, for instance), NTFS allocates another run for the additional data. Attributes whose values are stored in runs rather than in the MFT are called *nonresident attributes*. The file system decides whether a particular attribute is resident or nonresident; the location of the data is transparent to the process accessing it.

When an attribute is nonresident, as the data attribute for a large file might be, its header contains the information NTFS needs to locate the attribute's value on the disk. Figure 3-9 on the next page shows a nonresident data attribute stored in two runs.

Standard Information	File Name	Security Descriptor	Index Root	
			index of files	
			f1, f2, f3, . . .	empty

Figure 3-8. MFT File Record for a Small Directory

---

2. 4 KB for a 4-KB cluster size.

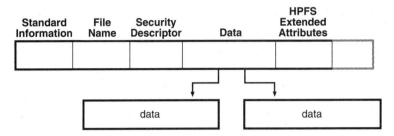

Figure 3-9. MFT File Record for a Large File with Two Data Runs

Among the standard attributes, only those that can grow can be nonresident. For files, the attributes that can grow are the security descriptor, the data, the attribute list (not shown in Figure 3-9), and the HPFS extended attributes (EAs). The standard information and file name attributes are always resident.

A large directory can also have nonresident attributes (or parts of attributes), as Figure 3-10 shows. In this example, the MFT file record doesn't have enough room to store the index of files that make up this large directory. A part of the index is stored in the index root attribute, and the rest of the index is stored in nonresident runs called *index buffers*. The index root, index allocation, and bitmap attributes are shown here in a simplified form. They are described in more detail later. The standard information and file name attributes are always resident. The header and at least part of the value of the index root attribute are also resident for directories.

When a file's (or a directory's) attributes can't fit in an MFT file record and separate allocations are needed, NTFS keeps track of the runs by means of *virtual cluster numbers* (VCNs). Logical cluster numbers (LCNs), described in Section 3.1, represent the sequence of clusters on an entire volume from

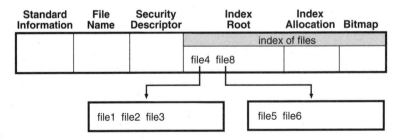

Figure 3-10. MFT File Record for a Large Directory with a Nonresident File Name Index

0 through *n*. VCNs number the clusters belonging to a particular file from 0 through *m*. For example, the clusters in the runs of a nonresident data attribute are numbered as shown in Figure 3-11.

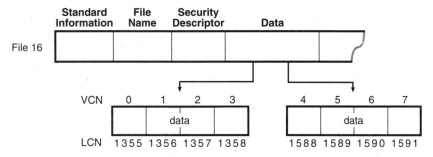

Figure 3-11. Virtual Cluster Numbers (VCNs) for a Nonresident Data Attribute

If this file had more than two runs, the numbering of the third run would start with VCN 8. As Figure 3-12 shows, the data attribute header contains VCN-to-LCN mappings for the two runs shown, which allows NTFS to easily find the allocations on the disk.

Figure 3-12 shows data runs, but other attributes can be stored in runs if there isn't enough room in the MFT file record to contain them. And if a particular file has too many attributes to fit in the MFT record, a second

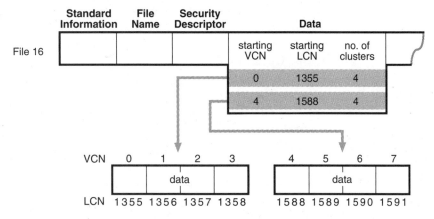

Figure 3-12. VCN-to-LCN Mappings for a Nonresident Data Attribute

MFT record is used to contain the additional attributes (or attribute headers for nonresident attributes). In this case, the attribute called the attribute list, which we saw in Figure 3-6 back on page 23, is added. The attribute list attribute contains the name and type code of each of the file's attributes and the file reference of the MFT record where the attribute is located. The attribute list attribute is provided for those cases in which a file grows so large or so fragmented that a single MFT record can't contain the multitude of VCN-to-LCN mappings needed to find all of its runs. NTFS needs this attribute so rarely that special dysfunctional programs had to be written to test the NTFS code that implements attribute lists.

3.3   File Name Indexing

In NTFS, a file directory is simply an index of file names—that is, a collection of file names (along with their file references) organized in a particular way for quick access. To create a directory, NTFS indexes the file name attributes of the files in the directory. The MFT record for the root directory of a volume is shown in Figure 3-13.

Conceptually, an MFT entry for a directory contains in its index root attribute a sorted list of the files in the directory. However, for large directories, the file names are actually stored in index buffers, runs of either 2 KB or the cluster size—whichever is larger—that contain and organize the file names. Index buffers implement a *b+ tree* data structure, which minimizes the number of disk accesses needed to find a particular file, especially for large directories. The index root attribute contains the first level of the b+ tree (root subdirectories) and points to index buffers containing the next level (more subdirectories, perhaps, or files). The index allocation attribute maps the VCNs of the index buffer runs to the LCNs that indicate where the index buffers reside on the disk.

Figure 3-13 shows only file names in the index root attribute and the index buffers (*file6*, for example), but each entry in an index also contains the file reference in the MFT where the file is described, and time stamp and file size information for the file. NTFS duplicates the time stamp and file size information from the file's MFT record. This technique, which is used by the FAT file system, HPFS, and NTFS, requires updated information to be written in two places. However, it is a significant speed optimization for directory browsing because it enables the file system to display each file's time stamps and size without opening every file in the directory.

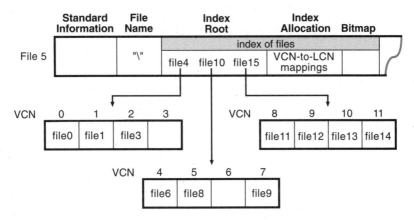

Figure 3-13. File Name Index for a Volume's Root Directory

The index allocation attribute contains the VCN-to-LCN mappings for the index buffers, and the bitmap attribute keeps track of which VCNs in the index buffers are in use and which are free. Figure 3-13 shows one file entry per VCN (that is, per cluster), but actually file name entries are packed into each cluster. Each 2-KB index buffer can contain about 15 file name entries (3 or 4 per cluster for a 512-byte cluster).

The b+ tree data structure (also used by HPFS) is a type of balanced tree that is ideal for organizing sorted data stored on a disk because it minimizes the number of disk accesses needed to find an entry. In the MFT, a directory's index root attribute contains several file names that act as indexes into the second level of the b+ tree. Each file name in the index root attribute has an optional pointer associated with it that points to an index buffer. The index buffer it points to contains file names with lexicographic values less than its own. In Figure 3-13, for example, *file4* is a first-level entry in the b+ tree. It points to an index buffer containing file names that are (lexicographically) less than itself—the file names *file0*, *file1*, and *file3*.

Storing the file names in b+ trees provides several benefits. Directory lookups are fast because the file names are stored in a sorted order. And when higher-level software enumerates the files in a directory, NTFS returns already-sorted names. Finally, because b+ trees tend to grow wide rather than deep, NTFS's fast lookup times don't degrade as directories get large.

NTFS currently indexes only the file name attribute, but later versions of the file system might allow applications to both create new attributes and index them. If the author of a file were added as an attribute, for example, NTFS could maintain b+ trees of files collated by author.

3.4 NTFS Metadata Files and the Boot File

In NTFS, all data stored on a volume is contained in a file, including the data structures used to locate and retrieve files, the bootstrap data, and the bitmap that records the allocation state of the entire volume (the NTFS metadata). Storing everything in files allows the data to be easily located and maintained by the file system, and each separate file can be protected by a security descriptor. In addition, if a particular part of the disk goes bad, NTFS can relocate the metadata files to prevent the disk from becoming inaccessible.

As noted earlier, the MFT contains a record for every file on the disk, including one for the MFT file itself. A file record in the MFT contains either all the attributes for the file or the VCN-to-LCN mappings that indicate where on the disk the values of the file's nonresident attributes are located. The location of the MFT file records for NTFS metadata files is illustrated in Figure 3-14.

When it first accesses a volume, NTFS must *mount* it—that is, prepare it for use. To mount the volume, NTFS looks in the boot file (described below) to find the physical disk address of the MFT. The MFT's own file record is the first entry in the table; the second file record points to a file located in the middle of the disk that contains a copy of the first 16 rows of the MFT. This partial copy of the MFT is used to locate metadata files if part of the MFT file can't be read for some reason.

Once NTFS finds the file record for the MFT, it obtains the VCN-to-LCN mapping information in the record's data attribute, decompresses it, and stores it in memory. This mapping information tells NTFS where the runs composing the MFT are located on the disk. NTFS then decompresses the MFT records for several more metadata files and opens the files. Next, NTFS performs its file system recovery operation (described in Section 4.3), and finally, it opens its remaining metadata files. The volume is now ready for user access.

As the system runs, NTFS writes to another important metadata file, the *log file*. NTFS uses the log file to record all operations that affect the NTFS volume structure, including file creation or any commands, such as Copy, that alter the directory structure. The log file is used to recover an NTFS volume after a system failure.

Another entry in the MFT is reserved for the root directory (also known as "\"). Its file record contains an index of the files and directories stored in the root of the NTFS directory structure. When NTFS is first asked

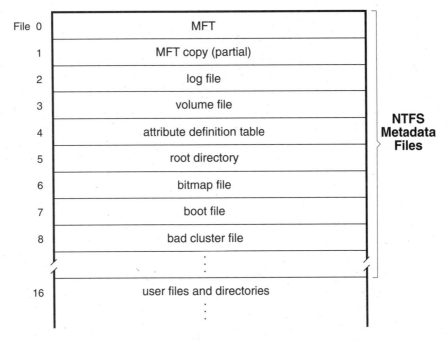

Figure 3-14. File Records for NTFS Metadata Files in the MFT

to open a file, it begins its search for the file in the root directory's file record. After opening a file, NTFS stores the file's MFT file reference so that it can directly access the file's MFT record when it reads and writes the file later.

NTFS records the allocation state of the volume in the *bitmap file*. The data attribute for the bitmap file contains a bitmap, each of whose bits represents a cluster on the volume, identifying whether the cluster is free or has been allocated to a file.

Another important system file is the *boot file,* which stores the Windows NT bootstrap code. In order for the system to boot, the bootstrap code must be located at a specific disk address. During formatting, however, the Format utility defines this area as a file by creating a file record for it. Creating the boot file allows NTFS to adhere to its rule of making everything on the disk a file. The boot file as well as NTFS metadata files can be individually protected by means of the security descriptors that are applied to all Windows NT objects. Using this "everything on the disk is a file" model also means that the bootstrap can be modified by normal file I/O, although the boot file is currently protected from editing.

NTFS also maintains a *bad cluster file* for recording any bad spots on the disk volume and a file known as the *volume file,* which contains the volume name, the version of NTFS for which the volume is formatted, and a bit that when set signifies that a disk corruption has occurred and must be repaired by the Chkdsk utility (see Section 5.3). Finally, NTFS maintains a file containing an *attribute definition table* that defines the attribute types supported on the volume and indicates whether they can be indexed, recovered during a system recovery operation, and so on.

CHAPTER FOUR

RECOVERABILITY

The most important feature of NTFS is undoubtedly its failure recovery capability. A recoverable file system ensures that if a power failure or a catastrophic system failure occurs, no file system operations (transactions) will be left incomplete and the structure of the disk volume will remain intact without the need to run a disk repair utility.[1] NTFS recoverability increases the overall reliability of Windows NT, a boon for corporate and other high-end customers. Windows NT file system recovery actually exceeds current corporate expectations for file system reliability, and NTFS provides this extra level of stability with little sacrifice of performance. Recoverability is a prerequisite for transaction-processing applications and for an attribute-indexing facility.

NTFS uses a transaction-based logging scheme to implement recoverability. This strategy ensures a full disk recovery that is also extremely fast (on the order of seconds) for even the largest disks. NTFS limits its recovery procedures to file system data to ensure that at the very least the user will never lose a volume because of a corrupted file system; however, user data is not guaranteed to be fully updated if a crash occurs. The decision not to implement user file recovery represents a trade-off between a fully fault tolerant file system and one that provides optimum performance for all file operations. User file recovery could be implemented as an extension to NTFS.

The first section of this chapter describes the evolution of file system reliability as a context for an introduction to recoverable file systems. The second section details the transaction-logging scheme NTFS uses to record

---

1. NTFS includes a Chkdsk utility that can be used to repair catastrophic disk corruption caused by I/O errors (bad disk sectors, electrical anomalies, or disk failures, for example) or software bugs. With the NTFS recovery capabilities in place, Chkdsk is rarely needed.

modifications to file system data structures, and the third section explains how NTFS recovers a volume if the system fails.

4.1 Evolution of File System Design

The development of a recoverable file system can be seen as a step forward in the evolution of file system design. Until now, there have been two common techniques for constructing a file system's I/O and caching support: *careful write* and *lazy write*. The file systems developed for Digital Equipment Corporation's VAX/VMS and some other proprietary operating systems employ a careful write algorithm, while OS/2 HPFS and most UNIX file systems use a lazy write file system scheme.

Careful write and lazy write file systems are prevalent on personal computer, minicomputer, and mainframe operating systems, but recoverable file systems are relatively new. Before NTFS, they appeared primarily on research systems and a few specialized real-time or fault tolerant systems. Windows NT is one of the first commercial operating systems to provide a recoverable file system.

The next two subsections briefly review the two types of file systems most commonly used today and their intrinsic trade-offs between safety and performance. The third subsection describes NTFS's recoverable approach and how it differs from the two other strategies.

4.1.1 Careful Write File Systems

When an operating system crashes or loses power, I/O operations in progress are immediately, and often prematurely, interrupted. Depending on what I/O operation or operations were in progress and how far along they were, such an abrupt halt can produce inconsistencies in a file system. An inconsistency in this context is a file system corruption—a file name appears in a directory listing, for instance, but the file system doesn't know the file is there or can't access the file. The worst file system corruptions can leave an entire volume inaccessible.

A careful write file system doesn't try to prevent file system inconsistencies. Rather, it orders its write operations so that, at worst, a system crash will produce predictable, noncritical inconsistencies, which the file system can fix at its leisure.

When any kind of file system receives a request to update the disk, it must perform several suboperations before the update will be complete. In a file system that uses the careful write strategy, the suboperations are always written to disk serially. When allocating disk space for a file, for example, the file system first sets some bits in its bitmap and then allocates the space to the file. If the power fails immediately after the bits are set, the careful write file system loses access to some disk space—to the space represented by the set bits—but existing data is not corrupted.

Serializing write operations also means that I/O requests are filled in the order in which they are received. If one process allocates disk space and shortly thereafter another process creates a file, a careful write file system completes the disk allocation before it starts to create the file because interleaving the suboperations of the two I/O requests could result in an inconsistent state.[2]

The main advantage of a careful write file system is that in the event of a failure the volume stays consistent and usable without the need to immediately run a slow volume repair utility. Such a utility is needed to correct the predictable, nondestructive disk inconsistencies that occur as the result of a system failure, but the utility can be run at a convenient time, typically when the system is rebooted.

4.1.2 Lazy Write File Systems

A careful write file system sacrifices speed for the safety it provides. A lazy write file system improves performance by using a "write-back" caching strategy; that is, it writes file modifications to the cache and flushes the contents of the cache to disk in an optimized way, usually as a background activity.[3]

The performance improvements associated with the lazy write caching technique take several forms. First, the overall number of disk writes is reduced. Because serialized, immediate disk writes aren't required, the contents of a buffer can be modified several times before they are written to disk. Second, the speed of servicing application requests is greatly increased because the file system can return control to the caller without waiting for disk writes to be completed. Finally, the lazy write strategy ignores the inconsistent intermediate states on a file volume that can result when the suboperations of two or more I/O requests are interleaved. It is thus easier to make the file system multithreaded, allowing more than one I/O operation to be in progress at a time.

---

2. The MS-DOS FAT file system uses a "write-through" algorithm that causes disk modifications to be immediately written to the disk. Unlike the careful write approach, the write-through technique does not require the file system to order its writes to prevent inconsistencies.

3. On Windows NT, both the FAT file system and HPFS are implemented as lazy write file systems—they write disk modifications to the cache. The cache manager, in turn, uses a lazy write scheme to optimize disk writes for all Windows NT file systems.

The disadvantage of the lazy write technique is that it creates intervals during which a volume is in too inconsistent a state to be corrected by the file system. Consequently, lazy write file systems must keep track of the volume's state at all times. HPFS, for example, sets a bit called the *dirty bit* during these intervals to indicate that the volume is in an inconsistent state. If the operating system crashes while the volume is "dirty," the volume must be reconstructed by means of the Chkdsk volume repair utility. In fact, because it generally cannot be known whether the volume was actually inconsistent at the time of a system crash, it is necessary to run Chkdsk after every reboot when the dirty bit is set. How long the HPFS volume repair takes depends on how big the disk is and how much damage it has sustained.

Although a disk repair can always produce a consistent volume, the volume might not always be repaired to the user's satisfaction. The HPFS Chkdsk utility sometimes has difficulty determining which directory a newly created file belongs to, for instance, and puts the new file in a catchall "found" directory. If the volume is severely corrupted, some files might be corrupted beyond reconstruction and will simply be lost. In general, lazy write file systems gain a performance advantage over careful write systems—at the expense of greater risk and user inconvenience if the system fails.

4.1.3 Recoverable File Systems

A recoverable file system tries to exceed the safety of a careful write file system while achieving the performance of a lazy write file system. A recoverable file system ensures volume consistency by using logging techniques originally developed for transaction processing. If the operating system crashes, the recoverable file system restores consistency by executing a recovery procedure that accesses information that has been stored in a log file. Because the file system has logged its disk writes, the recovery procedure takes only seconds, regardless of the size of the volume.

The NTFS recovery procedure is exact, guaranteeing that the volume will be restored to a consistent state. None of the inadequate restorations associated with lazy write file systems can happen with NTFS.

A recoverable file system incurs some costs for the safety it provides. Every transaction that alters the volume structure requires that one record be written to the log file for each of the transaction's suboperations. This logging overhead is ameliorated by the file system's "batching" of log records—writing many records to the log file in a single I/O operation. In addition, the recoverable file system can employ the optimization techniques of a lazy write file system. It can even increase the length of the intervals between cache flushes because the file system can be recovered if the system crashes before the cache changes have been flushed to disk. This gain over the caching performance of lazy write file systems makes up for, and often exceeds, the overhead of the recoverable file system's logging activity.

Neither careful write nor lazy write file systems guarantee protection of user file data. If the system crashes while an application is writing a file, the file can be lost or corrupted. Worse, the crash can corrupt a lazy write file system, destroying existing files or even rendering an entire volume inaccessible.

NTFS implements several strategies that improve its reliability over the reliability of the traditional file systems. First, NTFS recoverability guarantees that the volume structure will not be corrupted, so all files will remain accessible after a system failure.

Second, although NTFS does not currently guarantee protection of user data in the event of a system crash—some changes can be lost from the cache—applications can take advantage of the NTFS write-through and cache-flushing capabilities to ensure that file modifications are recorded on disk at appropriate intervals. Both *cache write-through*—forcing write operations to be immediately recorded on disk—and *cache flushing*—forcing cache contents to be written to disk—are efficient operations. NTFS doesn't have to do extra disk I/O to flush modifications to several different file system data structures because changes to the data structures are recorded—in a single write operation—in the log file; if a failure occurs and cache contents are lost, the file system modifications can be recovered from the log. Furthermore, unlike HPFS or the FAT file system, NTFS guarantees that user data will be consistent and available immediately after a write-through operation or a cache flush, even if the system subsequently fails.

Finally, NTFS has all the underpinnings to support logging for user files in the future. In lieu of user data logging, users who require an added measure of data reliability can use FtDisk, the Windows NT fault tolerant disk driver, to set up and maintain redundant data storage. (See Chapter Five, "Volume Management and Fault Tolerance," for more information about data redundancy.)

4.2 Logging

NTFS provides file system recoverability by means of a transaction-processing technique called *logging*. In NTFS logging, the suboperations of any transaction that alters important file system data structures are recorded in a log file before they are carried through on the disk. That way, if the system crashes, partially completed transactions can be redone or undone when the system comes back online. In NTFS, a *transaction* is defined as an I/O operation that alters file system data or changes the volume's directory structure. Such I/O operations include writing to the disk or deleting a file and may be made up of several suboperations.

There are two important components of the NTFS logging facilities: the *log file* itself and the *log file service* (LFS). The log file is a system file created by the Format command, and the LFS is a series of kernel-mode routines that NTFS uses to access the log file. Separating the LFS from the rest of the file system will allow other system components or future application software to create separate log files to implement application-level recoverability such as that used in transaction processing.

4.2.1 Log File Service (LFS)

Although designed to provide logging and recovery services for more than one client, the LFS is initially available only to file systems, through kernel-mode interfaces. The caller—NTFS in this case—passes the LFS a pointer to an open file object, which specifies a log file to be accessed. The LFS either initializes a new log file or calls the Windows NT cache manager to access the existing log file through the cache, as shown in Figure 4-1.

The LFS divides the log file into two regions: a *restart area* and an "infinite" *logging area,* as shown in Figure 4-2.

NTFS calls the LFS to read and write the restart area. NTFS uses the restart area to store context information such as the location in the logging

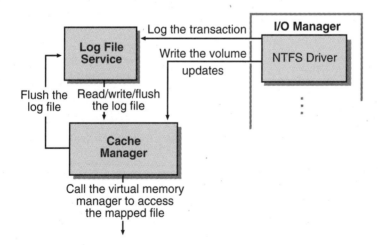

Figure 4-1. Log File Service (LFS)

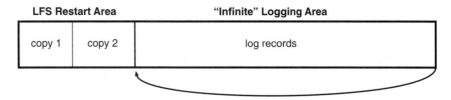

Figure 4-2. Log File

area at which NTFS will begin to read during recovery after a system failure. The LFS maintains a second copy of the restart data in case the first becomes corrupted or otherwise inaccessible. The remainder of the log file is the logging area, which contains transaction records NTFS writes in order to recover a volume in the event of a system failure. The LFS makes the log file appear infinite by reusing it circularly (while guaranteeing that it does not overwrite information it needs). The LFS uses *logical sequence numbers* (LSNs) to identify records written to the log file. As the LFS cycles through the file, it increases the values of the LSNs. The number of possible LSNs is so large as to be virtually infinite.

NTFS never reads transactions from or writes transactions to the log file directly. The LFS provides services NTFS calls to open the log file, write log records, read log records in forward or backward order, flush log records up to a particular LSN, or set the beginning of the log file to a higher LSN. During recovery, NTFS calls the LFS to read forward through the log records in order to redo any transactions that were recorded in the log file but were not flushed to disk at the time of the system failure. NTFS calls the LFS to read backward through the log records in order to undo, or roll back, any transactions that weren't completely logged before the crash. NTFS calls the LFS to set the beginning of the log file to a record with a higher LSN when NTFS no longer needs the older transaction records in the log file.

Here's how the system guarantees that the volume can be recovered:

1. NTFS first calls the LFS to record in the (cached) log file any transactions that will modify the volume structure.

2. NTFS modifies the volume (also in the cache).

3. The cache manager calls the LFS to prompt the LFS to flush the log file to disk. (The LFS implements the flush by calling the cache manager back, telling it which pages of memory to flush. Refer back to the calling sequence shown in Figure 4-1.)

4. After the cache manager flushes the log file to disk, it flushes the volume changes (the transactions themselves) to disk.

These steps ensure that if the file system modifications are ultimately unsuccessful, the corresponding transactions can be retrieved from the log file and can be either redone or undone as part of the file system recovery procedure.

File system recovery begins automatically the first time the volume is used after the system is rebooted. NTFS checks whether the transactions that were recorded in the log file before the crash were applied to the volume, and if they weren't, it redoes them. NTFS also guarantees that transactions not completely logged before the crash are undone so that they don't appear on the volume.

4.2.2 Log File

Before it modifies the volume, NTFS calls the LFS to record in the log file any transaction that will modify the NTFS volume structure. In doing so, NTFS employs a recovery-related technique known in transaction processing as *write-ahead logging*.

The LFS allows its clients to write any kind of record to their log files. NTFS writes several types of records, two of which—*update records* and *checkpoint records*—are described here.

4.2.2.1 Update Records

Update records are the most common type of record NTFS writes to the log file. Each update record contains these two kinds of information:

- *Redo information*—how to reapply one suboperation of a fully logged ("committed") transaction to the volume if a system failure occurs before the transaction is flushed from the cache.

- *Undo information*—how to reverse one suboperation of a transaction that was only partially logged ("not committed") at the time of a system failure.

Figure 4-3 shows three update records in the log file. Each record represents one suboperation of a transaction, creating a new file. The redo entry in each update record tells NTFS how to reapply the suboperation to the volume, and the undo entry tells NTFS how to roll back (undo) the suboperation.

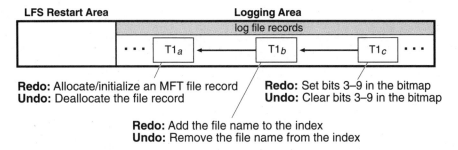

LFS Restart Area   **Logging Area**

Redo: Allocate/initialize an MFT file record   **Redo:** Set bits 3–9 in the bitmap
Undo: Deallocate the file record   **Undo:** Clear bits 3–9 in the bitmap

Redo: Add the file name to the index
Undo: Remove the file name from the index

Figure 4-3. Update Records in the Log File

After logging a transaction (in this example, by calling the LFS to write the three update records to the log file), NTFS performs the suboperations on the volume itself, in the cache. When it has finished updating the cache, NTFS writes another record to the log file, recording the entire transaction as complete—a suboperation known as *committing a transaction*. Once a transaction is committed, NTFS guarantees that the entire transaction will appear on the volume, even if the operating system subsequently fails.

When recovering after a system failure, NTFS reads through the log file and redoes each committed transaction. Although NTFS completed the committed transactions before the system failure, it doesn't know whether the cache manager flushed the volume modifications to disk in time. The updates might have been lost from the cache when the system failed. Therefore, NTFS executes the committed transactions again just to be sure that the disk is up to date.

After redoing the committed transactions during a file system recovery, NTFS locates all the transactions in the log file that were not committed at failure and rolls back (undoes) each suboperation that had been logged. In Figure 4-3, NTFS would first undo the $T1_c$ suboperation and then follow the backward pointer to $T1_b$ and undo that suboperation. It would continue to follow the backward pointers, undoing suboperations, until it reached the first suboperation in the transaction. By following the pointers, NTFS knows how many and which update records it must undo to roll back a transaction.

Redo and undo information can be expressed either physically or logically. Physical descriptions specify volume updates in terms of particular byte ranges on the disk that are to be changed, moved, and so on. Logical descriptions express updates in terms of operations such as "delete file A.DAT." As the lowest layer of software maintaining the file system structure, NTFS writes update records with physical descriptions. Transaction-processing or other application-level software might benefit from writing update records in logical terms, however, because logically expressed updates are more compact than physically expressed updates. Logical descriptions necessarily depend on NTFS to understand what operations such as deleting a file involve.

NTFS writes update records (usually several) for each of the following transactions:

- Creating a file
- Deleting a file
- Extending a file
- Truncating a file
- Setting file information
- Renaming a file
- Changing the security applied to a file

The redo and undo information in an update record must be carefully designed because while NTFS undoes a transaction, recovers from a system failure, or even operates normally, it might try to redo a transaction that has already been done or, conversely, to undo a transaction that never occurred or that has already been undone. Similarly, NTFS might try to redo or undo a transaction consisting of several update records, only some of which are complete on disk. The format of the update records must ensure that executing redundant redo or undo operations is *idempotent,* that is, has a neutral effect: for example, setting a bit that is already set has no effect, but toggling a bit that has already been toggled does. The file system must also handle intermediate volume states correctly.

4.2.2.2 Checkpoint Records

In addition to update records, NTFS periodically writes a checkpoint record to the log file, as illustrated in Figure 4-4.

A checkpoint record helps NTFS determine what processing would be needed to recover a volume if a crash were to occur immediately. Using information stored in the checkpoint record, NTFS knows, for instance, how far back in the log file it must go to begin its recovery. After writing a checkpoint record, NTFS stores the LSN of the record in the restart area so that it can quickly find its most recently written checkpoint record when it begins file system recovery after a crash occurs.

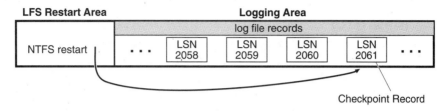

Figure 4-4. Checkpoint Record in the Log File

Although the LFS presents the log file to NTFS as if it were infinitely large, it isn't. The generous size of the log file and the frequent writing of checkpoint records (an operation that usually frees up space in the log file) make the possibility of the log file's filling up a remote one. Nevertheless, the LFS accounts for this possibility by tracking several numbers:

■ The available log space

■ The amount of space needed to write an incoming log record and to undo the write, should that be necessary

■ The amount of space needed to roll back all active (noncommitted) transactions, should that be necessary

If the log file doesn't contain enough available space to accommodate the total of the last two items, the LFS returns a "log file full" error and NTFS raises an exception. The NTFS exception handler rolls back the current transaction and places it in a queue to be restarted later.

To free up space in the log file, NTFS must momentarily halt I/O activity on the system. To do so, NTFS blocks file creation and deletion and then requests exclusive access to all open files. Gradually, active transactions either are completed successfully or receive the "log file full" exception. NTFS rolls back and queues the transactions that receive the exception.

Once it has halted I/O activity by acquiring exclusive access to all the open files, NTFS calls the cache manager to flush unwritten data to disk, including unwritten log file data. After everything is safely flushed to disk, NTFS no longer needs the data in the log file. It resets the beginning of the log file to the current position, making the log file "empty." Then it restarts the queued transactions. Beyond the short pause in I/O processing, the "log file full" error has no effect on executing programs.

This scenario is one example of how NTFS uses the log file not only for file system recovery but also for error recovery during normal operation. Error recovery is revisited in the next section.

4.3 Recovery

NTFS automatically performs a disk recovery the first time a program accesses an NTFS volume after the system has been booted. (If no recovery is needed, the process is trivial.) Recovery depends on two tables NTFS maintains in memory:

- The *transaction table* keeps track of transactions that have been started but that are not yet committed. The suboperations of these active transactions must be removed from the disk during recovery.

- The *dirty page table* records which pages in the cache contain modifications to the file system structure that have not yet been written to disk. This data must be flushed to disk during recovery.[4]

NTFS writes a checkpoint record to the log file once every 5 seconds. Just before it does, it calls the LFS to store a current copy of the transaction table and of the dirty page table in the log file. NTFS then records in the checkpoint record the logical sequence numbers (LSNs) of the log records containing the copied tables. When recovery begins after a system failure, NTFS calls the LFS to locate the log records containing the most recent checkpoint record and the most recent copies of the transaction and dirty page tables. It then copies the tables to memory.

The log file usually contains more update records following the last checkpoint record. These update records represent volume modifications that occurred after the last checkpoint record was written. NTFS must update the transaction and dirty page tables to include these operations. After updating the tables, NTFS uses the tables and the contents of the log file to update the volume itself.

To effect its volume recovery, NTFS scans the log file three times, loading the file into memory during the first pass to minimize disk I/O. Each pass has a particular purpose:

1. Analysis

2. Redoing transactions

3. Undoing transactions

---

4. For more information about Windows NT virtual memory, see *Inside Windows NT*, Chapter 6, "The Virtual Memory Manager."

4.3.1 Analysis Pass

During the *analysis pass*, as shown in Figure 4-5, NTFS scans forward in the log file from the beginning of the last checkpoint operation in order to find update records and use them to update the transaction and dirty page tables it copied to memory. Note in the figure that the checkpoint operation stores three records in the log file and that update records might be interspersed among these records. NTFS therefore must start its scan at the beginning of the checkpoint operation.

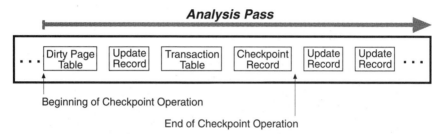

Figure 4-5. Analysis Pass

Each update record that appears in the log file after the checkpoint operation begins represents a modification to either the transaction table or the dirty page table. If an update record is a "transaction committed" record, for example, the transaction the record represents must be removed from the transaction table. Similarly, if the update record is a "page update" record that modifies a file system data structure, the dirty page table must be updated to reflect that change.

Once the tables are up to date in memory, NTFS scans the tables to determine the LSN of the oldest update record that logs an operation that has not been carried out on disk. The transaction table contains the LSNs of the noncommitted (incomplete) transactions, and the dirty page table contains the LSNs of records in the cache that have not been flushed to disk. The LSN of the oldest record that NTFS finds in these two tables determines where the redo pass will begin. If the last checkpoint record is older, however, NTFS will start the redo pass there instead.

4.3.2 Redo Pass

During the *redo pass*, as shown in Figure 4-6 on the next page, NTFS scans forward in the log file from the LSN of the oldest record it has found in the analysis pass. It looks for "page update" records, which contain volume modifications that were written before the system failure but that might not have been flushed to disk. NTFS redoes these updates in the cache.

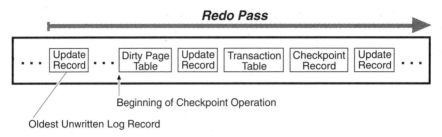

Figure 4-6. Redo Pass

When NTFS reaches the end of the log file, it has updated the cache with the necessary volume modifications and the cache manager's "lazy writer" can begin writing cache contents to disk in the background.

4.3.3 Undo Pass

After it completes the redo pass, NTFS begins its *undo pass,* in which it rolls back any transactions that weren't committed when the system failed. Figure 4-7 shows two transactions in the log file; transaction 1 was committed before the power failure, but transaction 2 was not. NTFS must undo transaction 2.

Suppose that transaction 2 created a file, an operation that comprises three suboperations, each with its own update record. The update records of a transaction are linked by backward pointers in the log file because they are usually not contiguous.

The NTFS transaction table lists the LSN of the last-logged update record for each noncommitted transaction. In this example, the transaction

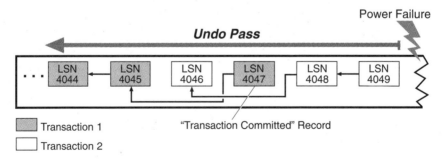

Figure 4-7. Undo Pass

table identifies LSN 4049 as the last update record logged for transaction 2. As shown from right to left in Figure 4-8, NTFS rolls back transaction 2.

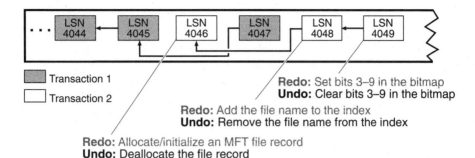

Figure 4-8. Undoing a Transaction

Each update record contains two kinds of information: how to redo a suboperation and how to undo it. After locating LSN 4049, NTFS finds the undo information and executes it, clearing bits 3 through 9 in its allocation bitmap. NTFS then follows the backward pointer to LSN 4048, which directs it to remove the new file name from the appropriate file name index. Finally, it follows the last backward pointer and deallocates the MFT file record reserved for the file, as the update record with the LSN 4046 specifies. Transaction 2 is now rolled back. If there are other noncommitted transactions to undo, NTFS follows the same procedure to roll them back. Because undoing transactions affects the volume's file system structure, NTFS must log the undo operations in the log file. After all, the power might fail again during the recovery, and NTFS would have to redo its undo operations!

When the undo pass of the recovery is complete, the volume has been restored to a consistent state.[5] At this point, NTFS flushes the cache changes to disk to ensure that the volume is up to date. NTFS then writes an "empty"

---

5. NTFS guarantees that recovery will return the volume to some preexisting consistent state, but not necessarily to the state that existed just before the system crash. NTFS can't make that guarantee because, for performance, it uses a "lazy commit" algorithm, which means that the log file is not immediately flushed to disk each time a "transaction committed" record is written. Instead, numerous transaction committed records are batched and written together, either when the cache manager calls the LFS to flush the log file to disk or when the LFS writes a checkpoint record (once every 5 seconds) to the log file. Another reason the recovered volume might not be completely up to date is that several parallel transactions might be active when the system crashes and some of their transaction committed records might make it to disk while others do not. The consistent volume that recovery produces includes all the volume updates whose transaction committed records made it to disk and none of the updates whose transaction committed records did not make it to disk.

LFS restart area to indicate that the volume is consistent and that no recovery need be done if the system should fail again immediately. Recovery is complete.

NTFS uses the log file to recover a volume after the system fails, but it also takes advantage of an important "freebie" it gets from logging transactions. File systems necessarily contain a lot of code devoted to recovering from file system errors that occur during the course of normal file I/O. Because NTFS logs each transaction that modifies the volume structure, it can use the log file to recover when a file system error occurs and thus can greatly simplify its error handling code. The "log file full" error described in Section 4.2.2.2 is one example of using the log file for error recovery.

Note that most I/O errors a program receives are not file system errors and therefore can't be resolved entirely by NTFS. When called to create a file, for example, NTFS might begin by creating a file record in the MFT and then enter the new file's name in a directory index. When it tries to allocate space for the file in its bitmap, however, it could discover that the disk is full and the create request can't be completed. In such a case, NTFS uses the information in the log file to undo the part of the operation it has already completed and to deallocate the data structures it reserved for the file. Then it returns a "disk full" error to the caller, which in turn must respond appropriately to the error.

CHAPTER FIVE

VOLUME MANAGEMENT AND FAULT TOLERANCE

The capabilities of NTFS are enhanced by underlying support from a Windows NT driver called FtDisk, the fault tolerant disk driver developed by Bob Rinne and Mike Glass. FtDisk lies above hard disk drivers in the I/O system's layered driver scheme and provides volume management capabilities, redundant data storage, and dynamic data recovery from bad sectors on SCSI (small computer system interface) disks.

Although FtDisk works with all of the Windows NT–supported file systems—NTFS, FAT, and HPFS—using it with NTFS provides the highest level of data integrity.

NTFS removes bad clusters from use when FtDisk is not installed in the system, and NTFS provides the equivalent of FtDisk's bad-sector recovery for non-SCSI hard disks. NTFS also monitors and detects corruption in file system data structures and uses FtDisk to recover its own data and to ensure its own reliability.

The first two sections of this chapter describe the volume management and data redundancy capabilities of FtDisk. The third section describes the additional features of NTFS that improve data reliability and recovery.

5.1 Volume Management Features

Although FtDisk is called the fault tolerant driver, it also implements some volume management features unrelated to fault tolerance. Volume sets and stripe sets don't provide data redundancy, but they do aid in organizing volumes and increasing I/O efficiency, respectively.

5.1.1 Volume Sets

A *volume set* is a single logical volume composed of a maximum of 32 areas of free space on one or more disks. The Windows NT Disk Administrator utility combines the areas into the volume set, which can then be formatted for any of the Windows NT–supported file systems. Figure 5-1 shows a 100-MB volume set identified by drive lette. D: that has been created from the last third of the first disk and the first third of the second.

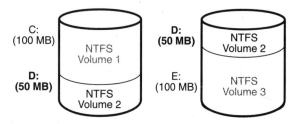

Figure 5-1. Volume Set

A volume set is useful for consolidating small areas of free disk space to create a larger volume or for creating a single, large volume out of two or more small disks. If the volume set has been formatted for NTFS, it can be extended to include additional free areas or additional disks without affecting the data already stored on the volume. This is one of the biggest benefits of describing all data on an NTFS volume as a file. NTFS can dynamically increase the size of a logical volume because the bitmap that records the allocation status of the volume is just another file—the bitmap file. The bitmap file can be extended to include any space added to the volume. Dynamically extending a FAT volume, on the other hand, would require the FAT itself to be extended, which would dislocate everything else on the disk.

FtDisk hides the physical configuration of disks from the file systems installed on Windows NT. NTFS, for example, views D: in Figure 5-1 as an ordinary 100-MB volume. NTFS consults its bitmap to determine what space in the volume is free for allocation. It then calls FtDisk to read or write data beginning at a particular byte offset on the volume. FtDisk views the physical sectors in the volume set as numbered sequentially from the first free area on the first disk to the last free area on the last disk. It determines which physical sector on which disk corresponds to the supplied byte offset.

5.1.2 Stripe Sets

A *stripe set* is a series of partitions, one partition per disk, that the Disk Administrator utility combines into a single logical volume. Figure 5-2 shows a stripe set consisting of three partitions, one on each of three disks. (A partition in a stripe set need not span an entire disk; the only restriction is that the partitions on each disk be the same size.)

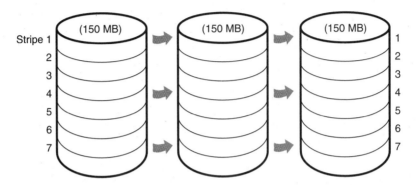

Figure 5-2. Stripe Set

To a file system, this stripe set appears to be a single 450-MB volume, but FtDisk optimizes data storage and retrieval times on the stripe set by distributing the volume's data among the physical disks. FtDisk accesses the physical sectors of the disks as if they were numbered sequentially in stripes across the disks, as illustrated in Figure 5-3.

Because each stripe is a relatively narrow 64 KB (a value chosen to prevent individual reads and writes from accessing two disks), the data tends to be distributed evenly among the disks. Stripes thus increase the probability

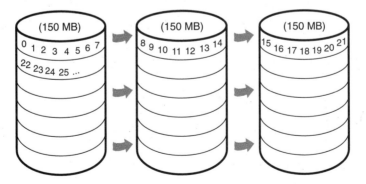

Figure 5-3. Logical Numbering of Physical Sectors on a Stripe Set

that multiple pending read and write operations will be bound for different disks. And because data on all three disks can be accessed simultaneously, latency time for disk I/O is often reduced, particularly on heavily loaded systems.

5.2 Fault Tolerant Volumes

Volume sets make managing disk volumes more convenient, and stripe sets spread the I/O load over multiple disks. These two volume-management features don't provide the ability to recover data if a disk fails, however. For data recovery, FtDisk implements three redundant storage schemes: mirror sets, duplex sets, and stripe sets with parity. Users can take advantage of these features through the Windows NT Disk Administrator utility.

5.2.1 Mirror Sets

In a *mirror set,* the contents of a partition on one disk are duplicated in an equal-size partition on another disk. A mirror set is shown in Figure 5-4.

When a program writes to C:, FtDisk writes the same data to the same location on the mirror partition. If the first disk or any of the data on its C: partition becomes unreadable because of a hardware or software failure, FtDisk automatically accesses the data from the mirror partition. A mirror set can be formatted for any of the Windows NT–supported file systems. The file system drivers remain independent and are not affected by FtDisk's mirroring activity.

Mirror sets can aid in I/O throughput on heavily loaded systems. When I/O activity is high, FtDisk balances its read operations between the primary partition and the mirror partition (accounting for the number of unfinished I/O requests pending from each disk). Two read operations can proceed simultaneously and thus theoretically finish in half the time. When a

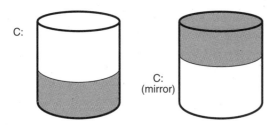

Figure 5-4. Mirror Set

file is modified, both partitions of the mirror set must be written, but disk writes are done asynchronously, so the performance of user-mode programs is generally not affected by the extra disk update.

5.2.2 Duplex Sets

A *duplex set* is a variant of a mirror set in which the mirror resides on a disk operated by a different disk controller. This configuration gives users of fault tolerant systems an added degree of assurance that if a disk controller (rather than just a disk) fails, the mirrored data remains available.

5.2.3 Stripe Sets with Parity

A *stripe set with parity* is a fault tolerant variant of a regular stripe set. Fault tolerance is achieved by reserving the equivalent of one disk for storing parity for each stripe. Figure 5-5 is a visual representation of a stripe set with parity.

In Figure 5-5, the parity for stripe 1 is stored on disk 1. It contains a byte-for-byte logical sum (XOR) of the first stripe on disks 2 and 3. The parity for stripe 2 is stored on disk 2, and the parity for stripe 3 is stored on disk 3. Rotating the parity across the disks in this way is an I/O optimization technique. Each time data is written to a disk, the parity bytes corresponding to the modified bytes must be recalculated and rewritten. If the parity were always written to the same disk, that disk would be busy continually and could become an I/O bottleneck.

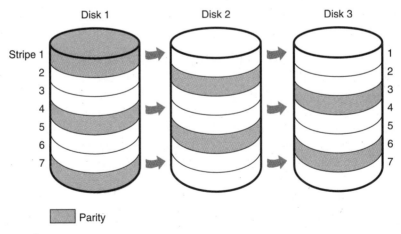

Figure 5-5. Stripe Set with Parity

Recovering a failed disk in a stripe set with parity relies on a simple arithmetic principle: in an equation with n variables, if you know the value of $n - 1$ of the variables, you can determine the value of the missing variable by subtraction. For example, in the equation $x + y = z$, where z represents the parity stripe, FtDisk computes $z - y$ to determine the contents of x; to find y, it computes $z - x$. FtDisk uses similar logic to recover lost data. If a disk in a stripe set with parity fails or if data on one disk becomes unreadable, FtDisk reconstructs the missing data by using the XOR operation (bitwise logical addition).

If disk 1 in Figure 5-5 fails, the contents of its stripes 2 and 5 are calculated by XOR-ing the corresponding stripes of disk 3 with the parity stripes on disk 2. The contents of stripes 3 and 6 are similarly determined by XOR-ing the corresponding stripes of disk 2 with the parity stripes on disk 3. At least three disks (or rather, three same-size partitions on three disks) are required to create a stripe set with parity.

5.2.4 Sector Sparing

Redundant data storage is used not only for recovering data after a complete disk failure but also for recovering data from a single physical sector that goes bad. In a technique called *sector sparing,* FtDisk uses its redundant data storage to dynamically replace lost data when a disk sector becomes unreadable. The sector-sparing technique exploits a feature of some hard disks, which provide a set of physical sectors reserved as "spares." If FtDisk receives a data error from the hard disk, it obtains a spare sector from the disk driver to replace the bad sector that caused the data error. FtDisk recovers the data that was on the bad sector (by either reading the data from a disk mirror or recalculating the data from a stripe set with parity) and copies it to the spare sector. FtDisk performs sector sparing dynamically, without intervention from the file system or the user, and sector sparing works with any Windows NT–supported file system on SCSI-based hard disks.

If a bad-sector error occurs and the hard disk doesn't provide spares, runs out of them, or is a non-SCSI-based disk, FtDisk can still recover the data. It recalculates the unreadable data by accessing a stripe set with parity, or it reads a copy of the data from a disk mirror. It then passes the data to the file system along with a warning status that only one copy of the data remains in a disk mirror or that one stripe is inaccessible in a stripe set with parity, and that data redundancy is therefore no longer in effect for that sector. It's up to the file system to respond to (or ignore) the warning. FtDisk will re-recover the data each time the file system tries to read from the bad sector.

5.3 NTFS Bad-Cluster Recovery

FtDisk can recover data from a bad sector on a fault tolerant volume, but if the hard disk doesn't use the SCSI protocol or runs out of spare sectors, FtDisk can't perform sector sparing to replace the bad sector. When the file system reads from the sector, FtDisk instead recovers the data and returns the warning to the file system that there is only one copy of the data.

The FAT and HPFS file systems don't respond to this FtDisk warning. Moreover, neither these file systems nor FtDisk keeps track of the bad sectors, so a user must run the Chkdsk or Format utility to prevent FtDisk from repeatedly recovering data for the file system. Both Chkdsk and Format are less than ideal for removing bad sectors from use. Chkdsk can take a long time to find and remove bad sectors, and Format wipes all the data off the partition it is formatting.

In the file system equivalent of FtDisk's sector sparing, NTFS dynamically replaces the cluster containing a bad sector and keeps track of the bad cluster so that it won't be reused.[1] NTFS performs these functions when FtDisk can't perform sector sparing or when FtDisk is not installed in the system. When FtDisk returns a bad-sector warning or when the hard disk driver returns a bad-sector error, NTFS allocates a new cluster to replace the one containing the bad sector. If FtDisk is present, NTFS copies the data that FtDisk has recovered into the new cluster to reestablish data redundancy.

Figure 5-6 on the next page shows an NTFS file record for a user file with a bad cluster in one of its data runs. When it receives a bad-sector error, NTFS reassigns the cluster containing the sector to its bad-cluster file. This prevents the bad cluster from being allocated to another file. NTFS then allocates a new cluster for the file and changes the file's VCN-to-LCN mappings to point to the new cluster. This procedure, known as *bad-cluster remapping*, is illustrated in Figure 5-7 on page 57. Cluster number 1357, which contains the bad sector, is replaced by a new cluster, number 1049.

---

1. As Chapter 3 pointed out, NTFS maintains portability by addressing logical clusters rather than physical sectors.

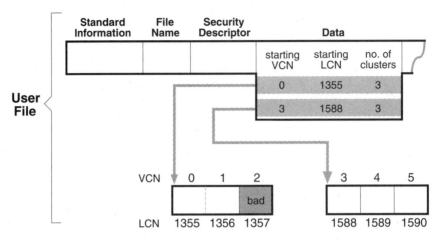

Figure 5-6. MFT Record for a User File with a Bad Cluster

Bad-sector errors are undesirable, but when they do occur, the combination of NTFS and FtDisk provides the best possible solution. If the bad sector is on a redundant volume, FtDisk recovers the data and replaces the sector if it can. If it can't replace the sector, it returns a warning to NTFS and NTFS replaces the cluster containing the bad sector.

If FtDisk is not loaded or if the volume is not configured as a redundant volume, the data in the bad sector can't be recovered. When the volume is formatted as a FAT or an HPFS volume and FtDisk can't recover the data, reading from the bad sector yields indeterminate results. If some of the file system's control structures reside in the bad sector, an entire file or group of files (or potentially, the whole disk) can be lost. At best, some data in the affected file (often, all the data in the file beyond the bad sector) is lost. Moreover, the FAT or HPFS file system is likely to reallocate the bad sector to the same or another file on the volume, causing the problem to resurface.

Like the other file systems, NTFS can't recover data from a bad sector without help from FtDisk. However, NTFS greatly contains the damage a bad sector can cause. If NTFS discovers the bad sector during a read operation, it remaps the cluster the sector is in, as shown in Figure 5-7. If the volume is not configured as a redundant volume, NTFS returns a data read error to the calling program. Although the data that was in that cluster is lost, the rest of the file—and the file system—remains intact; the calling program can respond appropriately to the data loss; and the bad cluster won't be reused in future allocations. If NTFS discovers the bad cluster on a write operation

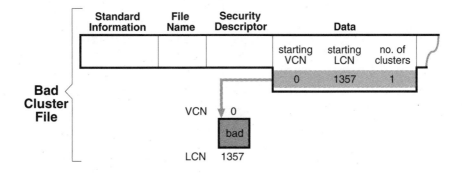

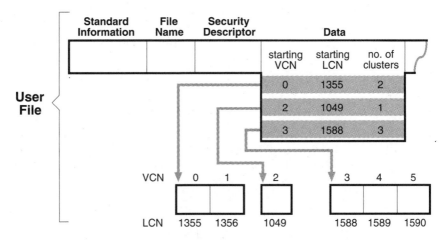

Figure 5-7. Bad-Cluster Remapping

rather than a read, NTFS remaps the cluster before writing, and thus loses no data and generates no error.

The same recovery procedures are followed if file system data is stored in a sector that goes bad. If the bad sector is on a redundant volume, NTFS replaces the cluster dynamically, using the data recovered by FtDisk. If the volume isn't redundant, the data can't be recovered and NTFS sets a bit in the volume file that indicates corruption on the volume. The NTFS Chkdsk utility checks this bit when the system is next rebooted, and if the bit is set, Chkdsk executes, fixing the file system corruption by reconstructing the NTFS metadata.

In rare instances, file system corruption can occur on even a fault tolerant disk configuration. A double error can destroy both file system data and the means to reconstruct it. If the system crashes while NTFS is writing the mirror copy of an MFT file record, of a file name index, or of the log file, for example, the mirror copy of such file system data might not be fully updated. If the system were rebooted and a bad-sector error occurred on the primary disk at exactly the same location as the incomplete write on the disk mirror, NTFS would be unable to recover the correct data from the disk mirror. NTFS implements a special scheme for detecting such corruptions in file system data. If it ever finds an inconsistency, it sets the corruption bit in the volume file, which causes Chkdsk to reconstruct the NTFS metadata when the system is next rebooted. Because file system corruption is rare on a fault tolerant disk configuration, Chkdsk is seldom needed. It is supplied as a safety precaution rather than as a first-line data recovery strategy.[2]

Figure 5-8 summarizes what happens when a sector goes bad on a disk volume formatted for one of the Windows NT–supported file systems according to various conditions that have been described in this chapter.

Note that if FtDisk is installed, if the volume on which the bad sector appears is a fault tolerant volume, and if the hard disk is one that supports sector sparing (and that hasn't run out of spare sectors), what file system you are using—FAT, HPFS, or NTFS—doesn't matter. FtDisk replaces the bad sector without the need for user or file system intervention.

If FtDisk is not installed or is installed on a hard disk that doesn't support sector sparing, the file system is responsible for replacing (remapping) the bad sector or—in the case of NTFS—the cluster in which the bad sector resides. Neither the FAT file system nor HPFS provides sector or cluster remapping. The benefits of NTFS cluster remapping are that bad spots in a file can be fixed without harm to the file (or harm to the file system, as the case may be) and that the bad cluster won't be reallocated to the same or another file.

---

2. Use of Chkdsk on NTFS is vastly different from its use on the FAT file system and on HPFS. Before writing anything to disk, both FAT and HPFS set the volume's "dirty bit" and then reset the bit after the modification is complete. If any I/O operation is in progress when the system crashes, the dirty bit is left set and Chkdsk runs when the system is rebooted. On NTFS, Chkdsk runs only when unexpected or unreadable file system data is found and NTFS can't recover the data from a redundant volume or from redundant file system structures on a single volume. (The system boot sector is duplicated, as are the parts of the MFT required for booting the system and running the NTFS recovery procedure. This redundancy ensures that NTFS will always be able to boot and recover itself.)

	FtDisk Installed...		FtDisk Not Installed...
	With a SCSI disk that has spare sectors	With a non-SCSI disk or a disk with no spare sectors[*]	With any kind of disk
Fault Tolerant Volume[†]	1. FtDisk recovers the data 2. FtDisk performs *sector sparing* (replaces the bad sector) 3. File system remains unaware of the error	1. FtDisk recovers the data 2. FtDisk sends the data and a bad-sector error to the file system 3. NTFS performs *cluster remapping*	N/A
Non-Fault-Tolerant Volume	1. FtDisk can't recover the data 2. FtDisk sends a bad-sector error to the file system 3. NTFS performs *cluster remapping* Data is lost[‡]	1. FtDisk can't recover the data 2. FtDisk sends a bad-sector error to the file system 3. NTFS performs *cluster remapping* Data is lost[‡]	1. Disk driver returns a bad-sector error to the file system 2. NTFS performs *cluster remapping* Data is lost[‡]

[*] In neither of these cases can FtDisk perform sector sparing: (1) hard disks that don't use the SCSI protocol have no standard interface for providing sector sparing; (2) some hard disks don't provide hardware support for sector sparing, and SCSI hard disks that do provide sector sparing can eventually run out of spare sectors if a lot of sectors go bad.

[†] A fault tolerant volume is one of the following: a mirror set, a duplex set, or a stripe set with parity.

[‡] In a write operation, no data is lost: NTFS remaps the cluster before the write.

Figure 5-8. Summary of FtDisk and NTFS Data Recovery Scenarios

CHAPTER SIX

DATA COMPRESSION

With MS-DOS versions 6.0 and 6.2, a new feature was implemented in the FAT file system: disk file compression. Called Doublespace, the compression utility effectively doubled the storage capacity of FAT-formatted disks, eliminating or at least postponing most users' need to upgrade their disk hardware. The files on a compressed volume are decompressed dynamically as a user reads from them and are written back to the disk in compressed form when a user writes to them.

After the first release of Windows NT, which did not include data compression, the NTFS team immediately began to investigate implementing NTFS file compression. In the design of compression software, a trade-off exists between the size of compressed files and the speed of compression and decompression. Doublespace sacrificed some speed in order to achieve smaller compressed files. It compressed bytes of data, packing them to the bit to shrink file size. For NTFS, Tom Miller and Gary Kimura opted to emphasize speed of decompression over file size and not to perform bit-level data manipulation.

They also hoped to implement fast lookups for read operations. With a Doublespace volume, the FAT file system had to access the disk at least three times to locate a compressed file. By using the VCN-to-LCN mappings described in Chapter 3, NTFS can locate a compressed file in one lookup operation—the same number of lookups it takes to find a noncompressed file.

In addition to emphasizing performance, the file system team wanted to provide flexibility by enabling users to select files for compression rather than requiring them to compress entire volumes. The ability to compress files selectively would permit system administrators, for example, to identify infrequently used or large files and compress just those files.

The following section introduces NTFS compression by examining the simple case of compressing sparse files. The second section extends the discussion to the compression of ordinary files.

6.1 Compressing a Sparse File

NTFS uses virtual cluster numbers (VCNs), from 0 through m, to enumerate the clusters of a file. Each VCN maps to a corresponding logical cluster number (LCN), which identifies the disk location of the cluster. Figure 6-1 illustrates the runs (disk allocations) of a normal, noncompressed file, including its VCNs and the LCNs they map to.

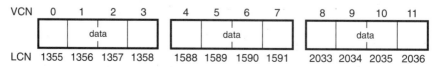

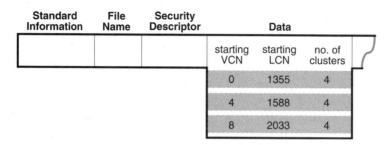

Figure 6-1. Runs of a Noncompressed File

This file is stored in three runs, each of which is 4 clusters long, for a total of 12 clusters. Figure 6-2 shows the master file table (MFT) record for this file. To save space, the MFT record's data attribute, which contains VCN-to-LCN mappings, records only one mapping for each run, rather than one for each cluster. Notice, however, that each VCN from 0 through 11 has a corresponding LCN associated with it. The first entry starts at VCN 0 and covers 4 clusters, the second entry starts at VCN 4 and covers 4 clusters, and so on. This entry format is typical for a noncompressed file.

Sparse files are files, often large, that contain only a small amount of nonzero data relative to their size. A sparse matrix stored on disk is one example of a sparse file. When a user selects an NTFS file for compression, one NTFS compression technique is to remove long strings of zeros from the file. If the file is sparse, it typically shrinks to occupy a fraction of the disk space it would otherwise require. On subsequent writes to the file, NTFS allocates space only for runs that contain nonzero data.

Standard Information	File Name	Security Descriptor	Data		
			starting VCN	starting LCN	no. of clusters
			0	1355	4
			4	1588	4
			8	2033	4

Figure 6-2. MFT Record for a Noncompressed File

Figure 6-3 depicts the runs of a compressed sparse file. Notice that certain ranges of the file's VCNs (16–31 and 64–127) have no disk allocations.

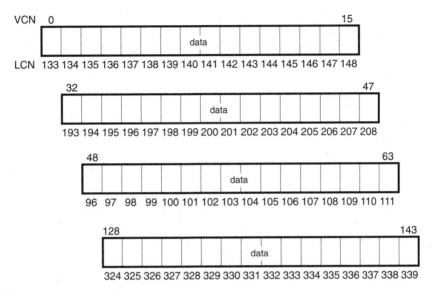

Figure 6-3. Runs of a Compressed Sparse File

The MFT record for this sparse file omits blocks of VCNs that contain zeros and therefore have no physical storage allocated to them. The first data entry in Figure 6-4, for example, starts at VCN 0 and covers 16 clusters. The second entry jumps to VCN 32 and covers 16 clusters.

When a program reads data from a compressed file, NTFS checks the MFT record to determine whether a VCN-to-LCN mapping covers the

Standard Information	File Name	Security Descriptor	Data		
			starting VCN	starting LCN	no. of clusters
			0	133	16
			32	193	16
			48	96	16
			128	324	16

Figure 6-4. MFT Record for a Compressed Sparse File

location being read. If the program is reading from an unallocated "hole" in the file, it means that the data in that part of the file consists of zeros, so NTFS returns zeros without accessing the disk. If a program writes non-zero data to a "hole," NTFS quietly allocates disk space and then writes the data. This technique is very efficient for sparse files that contain a lot of zero data.

6.2 Compressing Nonsparse Data

The example of compressing a sparse file in Section 6.1 is somewhat contrived. It describes "compression" for a case in which whole sections of a file are filled with zeros but the remaining data in the file wasn't affected by the compression. The data in most files is not sparse, but it can still be compressed by the application of a compression algorithm.

In NTFS, users can specify compression for individual files or for all the files in a directory. When it compresses a file, NTFS divides the file's unprocessed data into *compression units* 16 clusters long (equal to 8 KB for a 512-byte cluster). Certain sequences of data in a file might not compress much, if at all; so for each compression unit in the file, NTFS determines whether compressing the unit will save at least 1 cluster of storage. If compressing the unit won't free up at least 1 cluster, NTFS allocates a 16-cluster run and writes the data in that unit to disk without compressing it. If the data in a 16-cluster unit will compress to 15 or fewer clusters, NTFS allocates only the number of clusters needed to contain the compressed data and then writes it to disk. Figure 6-5 illustrates the compression of a file with four runs. The unshaded areas in this figure represent the actual storage locations that the file occupies after compression. The first, second, and fourth runs were compressed; the third run was not. Even with one noncompressed run, compressing this file saved 26 clusters of disk space, or 41 percent.[1]

When it writes data to a compressed file, NTFS ensures that each run begins on a virtual 16-cluster boundary. Thus, the starting VCN of each run is a multiple of 16 and the runs are no longer than 16 clusters. NTFS reads and writes at least one compression unit at a time when it accesses compressed files. However, when it writes compressed data, NTFS tries to store compression units in physically contiguous locations so that it can read them

---

1. Note that a compression unit need not be stored in physically contiguous clusters, although the diagrams in this chapter show contiguous LCNs. Runs that occupy non-contiguous clusters produce slightly more complicated MFT records than the one shown in Figure 6-6.

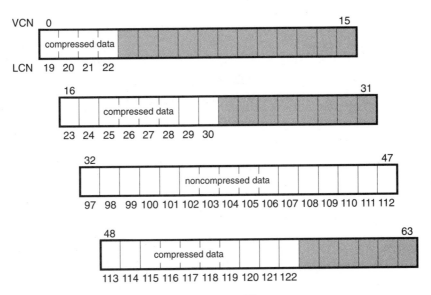

Figure 6-5. Data Runs of a Compressed File

all in a single I/O operation. The 16-cluster size of the NTFS compression unit was chosen to reduce internal fragmentation: the larger the compression unit, the less the overall disk space needed to store the data.[2] Figure 6-6 shows the MFT record for the compressed file shown in Figure 6-5.

One difference between this compressed file and the earlier example of a compressed sparse file is that three of the compressed runs in this file

Standard Information	File Name	Security Descriptor	Data		
			starting VCN	starting LCN	no. of clusters
			0	19	4
			16	23	8
			32	97	16
			48	113	10

Figure 6-6. MFT Record for a Compressed File

2. This 16-cluster compression unit size represents a trade-off between producing smaller compressed files and slowing read operations for programs that randomly access files. The equivalent of 16 clusters must be decompressed for each cache miss. (A cache miss is more likely to occur during random file access.)

are fewer than 16 clusters long. Reading this information from a file's MFT file record enables NTFS to know whether data in the file is compressed. Any run shorter than 16 clusters contains compressed data that NTFS must decompress when it first reads the data into the cache. A run that is exactly 16 clusters long does not contain compressed data and therefore requires no decompression.

If the data in a run has been compressed, NTFS decompresses the data into a scratch buffer and then copies it to the caller's buffer. NTFS also loads the decompressed data into the cache, which makes subsequent reads from the same run as fast as any other cached read. NTFS writes any updates to the file in the cache, leaving the lazy writer to compress and write the modified data to disk asynchronously. This strategy ensures that writing to a compressed file produces no more significant delay than writing to a non-compressed file would.

NTFS keeps disk allocations for a compressed file contiguous whenever possible. As the LCNs indicate, the first two runs of the compressed file shown in Figure 6-5 are physically contiguous, as are the last two. When two or more runs are contiguous, NTFS performs disk read-ahead, as it does with the data in other files. Because the reading and decompression of contiguous file data take place asynchronously before the program requests the data, subsequent read operations obtain the data directly from the cache, which greatly enhances read performance.

NTFS is designed so that the code that compresses files (the *compression engine*) is a replaceable module. This will allow NTFS to take advantage of new compression technology over time and to compress various kinds of files. Multimedia files, for example, require a different compression algorithm than text files do.

The two measures of success for data compression software are size and speed. In the size category, NTFS compression achieves excellent results. The early versions of Doublespace did a creditable job, compressing text files to approximately 40 percent of their original sizes and compressing executables and DLLs to 60 to 70 percent of their original sizes. Early versions of NTFS achieve even better compression figures: some files end up as much as 14 percent smaller than their Doublespace-compressed counterparts. Even though NTFS chose to trade off size in favor of speed, it still produces small file sizes because it uses a large "compression window"; that is, it sends 4 KB to the compression engine on each call. A large compression window yields more efficient compression for many compression algorithms.

In terms of speed, NTFS data compression is still under development. Executing the nonoptimized C version of the compression engine has not significantly slowed NTFS file I/O. After the NTFS compression engine has been rewritten in optimized assembly language, its developers expect compression and decompression to operate several times faster than they do now.

NTFS compression is performed only for user data, not for file system metadata, but that could change in future system releases.

MS-DOS FILE NAME GENERATION

Both NTFS and HPFS allow each file name in a path to be as many as 255 characters long. NTFS file names can contain Unicode characters as well as multiple periods and embedded spaces. The FAT file system is limited to 8 (non-Unicode) characters for its file names, followed by a period and a 3-character extension. Because of this limitation, MS-DOS clients accessing an HPFS-formatted disk can't view files with long names. The long names don't show up when the MS-DOS client issues a Dir command; nor do they show up when an MS-DOS–Windows client browses a file directory. Moreover, MS-DOS utilities such as Xcopy can't access files with long names. Businesses that operate OS/2 servers and use MS-DOS systems as clients therefore rarely take advantage of the long file name capability of HPFS.

Because Windows NT supports MS-DOS and MS-DOS–Windows clients, the NTFS developers decided that NTFS-created files should be visible and accessible to these clients, even if the files have names that are "illegal" for MS-DOS systems. Figure 7-1 on the next page provides a visual representation of the different *file namespaces* Windows NT supports and how they intersect.

The POSIX subsystem requires the biggest namespace of all the application execution environments that Windows NT supports, and therefore the NTFS namespace is equivalent to the POSIX namespace. The POSIX subsystem can create names that are not visible to Win32 and MS-DOS applications, including names with trailing periods and trailing spaces. Ordinarily, creating a file using the large POSIX namespace is not a problem because one would do that only if that file were intended to be used by the POSIX subsystem or by POSIX client systems.

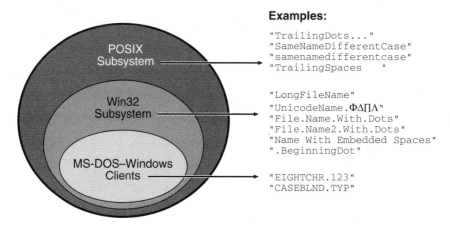

Examples:

```
"TrailingDots..."
"SameNameDifferentCase"
"samenamedifferentcase"
"TrailingSpaces    "
```

```
"LongFileName"
"UnicodeName.ΦΔΠΛ"
"File.Name.With.Dots"
"File.Name2.With.Dots"
"Name With Embedded Spaces"
".BeginningDot"
```

```
"EIGHTCHR.123"
"CASEBLND.TYP"
```

Figure 7-1. Windows NT File Namespaces

The relationship between 32-bit Windows (Win32) applications and MS-DOS–Windows applications is a much closer one, however. The Win32 area in Figure 7-1 represents file names that the Win32 subsystem can create on an NTFS volume but which MS-DOS and 16-bit Windows applications can't see. This group includes file names longer than the 8.3 format of MS-DOS names, those containing Unicode (international) characters, those with multiple period characters or a beginning period, and those with embedded spaces. When a file is created with such a name, NTFS automatically generates an alternate, MS-DOS-style, file name for the file. Windows NT displays these short names when a user is browsing in the File Manager with the View menu's All File Details option selected or when a user types the /x option with the Dir command.

The MS-DOS file names are fully functional aliases for the NTFS files and are stored in the same directory as the long file names. The Master File Table (MFT) record for a file with an auto-generated MS-DOS file name is shown in Figure 7-2.

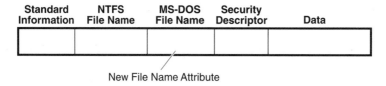

Standard Information	NTFS File Name	MS-DOS File Name	Security Descriptor	Data

New File Name Attribute

Figure 7-2. MFT File Record with an MS-DOS File Name Attribute

The NTFS name and the generated MS-DOS name are stored in the same file record and therefore refer to the same file. The MS-DOS name can be used to open, read from, write to, or copy the file. If a user renames the file using either the long file name or the short file name, the new name replaces both of the existing names.[1] If the new name is not a valid MS-DOS name, NTFS generates another MS-DOS name for the file.

Here's the algorithm NTFS currently uses to generate an MS-DOS name from a long file name:

1. Remove from the long name any characters that are illegal in MS-DOS names, including spaces and Unicode characters. Remove preceding and trailing periods. Remove all other embedded periods, except the last one.

2. Truncate the string before the period (if present) to six characters and append the string "~1". Truncate the string after the period (if present) to three characters.

3. Put the result in uppercase letters. MS-DOS is case-insensitive, and this step guarantees that NTFS won't generate a new name that differs from the old only in case.

4. If the generated name duplicates an existing name in the directory, increment the "~1" string.

Figure 7-3 on the next page shows the long Win32 file names from Figure 7-1 and their NTFS-generated MS-DOS versions. The current algorithm and the examples in Figure 7-3 should give users an idea of what NTFS-generated MS-DOS-style file names look like. Application developers shouldn't depend on this algorithm. It might change in the future.

---

1. POSIX hard links are implemented in a similar way. When a hard link to a POSIX file is created, NTFS adds another file name attribute to the file's MFT file record. The two situations differ in one regard, however. When a user deletes a POSIX file that has multiple names (hard links), the file record and the file remain in place. The file and its record are deleted only when the last file name (hard link) is deleted. If a file has both an NTFS name and an auto-generated MS-DOS name, however, a user can delete the file using either name and the file is immediately deleted.

Win32 Long Name	NTFS-Generated Short Name
LongFileName	LONGFI~1
UnicodeName.ΦΔΠΛ ·	UNICOD~1
File.Name.With.Dots	FILENA~1.DOT
File.Name2.With.Dots	FILENA~2.DOT
Name With Embedded Spaces	NAMEWI~1
.BeginningDot	BEGINN~1

Figure 7-3. NTFS-Generated File Names

CONCLUSION

As the introduction to this book observed, the NTFS team's most important goal was to create a file system that was not only reliable but also fast. Specifically, the goal was to achieve disk performance that would meet or exceed that of existing personal computer file systems.

Tom Miller's early contention that a recoverable file system does not have to sacrifice performance has held up well to scrutiny. Benchmark tests performed by various industry trade journals[1] show that NTFS I/O ranges from 1.5 to 8 times faster than I/O on Windows 3.1 (with and without SmartDrive) and OS/2 version 2.1. The results vary depending on hardware configuration and on whether the tested software is 16-bit or 32-bit code.

As trade journals have noted, the superlative performance of Windows NT disk I/O is not due solely to the implementation of NTFS. The performance achievement comes in large measure from synergy between NTFS and the Windows NT cache manager. Together, NTFS and the cache manager achieve I/O performance that easily exceeds that of other PC operating systems while providing an unprecedented level of reliability and high-end data storage features for desktop and server systems.

---

1. *Byte* and *PC Magazine*. See the bibliography.

GLOSSARY

analysis pass The first of three scans NTFS makes through the log file during file system recovery. During the analysis pass, NTFS scans forward from the last checkpoint record, using information in the log file's update records to update its in-memory tables. Compare *redo pass, undo pass*; see also *checkpoint record.*

API application programming interface.

application programming interface (API) A set of routines an application program calls to request and carry out lower-level services performed by an operating system.

atomic transaction A transaction whose multiple disk updates are treated as a single operation. See also *transaction.*

attribute definition table The NTFS file that defines the attribute types supported on a volume and whether they can be indexed, recovered during a file system recovery operation, and so on.

b+ tree A balanced tree data structure that grows wide rather than deep, thus minimizing the number of disk accesses needed to find a particular entry. NTFS stores file name indexes in a b+ tree structure. See also *index.*

bad-cluster file The NTFS file that keeps track of bad clusters—those containing bad sectors—on a volume.

bad-cluster remapping An NTFS feature in which the file system reassigns a cluster containing a bad sector to its bad-cluster file, preventing the cluster from being reallocated to another file. NTFS then allocates a new cluster and changes the file's VCN-to-LCN mappings to point to the new cluster. If the bad sector is located on a disk mirror or a stripe set with parity, NTFS also recovers the data that was on the bad sector and copies it to the new cluster. This cluster-remapping technique works on all types of hard disks. See also *sector sparing.*

base file record The first file record in the master file table (MFT) for a file that has multiple file records. The base file record is the record to which the file's file reference corresponds. See also *file record, file reference.*

bitmap file   The NTFS file that records the allocation state of a volume. The data attribute in the bitmap file's file record contains a bitmap, each of whose bits represents a cluster on the volume, identifying whether the cluster is free or has been allocated to a file.

boot file   The system file that stores the Windows NT bootstrap code.

cache flushing   Forcing cache contents to be written to disk.

cache manager   A component of the Windows NT executive that provides system-wide caching services. NTFS and other file system drivers call the cache manager to read and write cached files. The cache manager calls the virtual memory manager to map the cached files into virtual memory, read and write them, and flush modifications back to disk.

cache miss   A thread's attempt to access a part of a cached file that is not present in the cache. When the cache manager tries to copy the data to the user's buffer, a page fault occurs. The virtual memory manager, in turn, calls the appropriate file system driver to access the disk driver and copy the file contents from disk into the cache. See also *cache manager.*

cache write-through   The process of forcing each write operation to be immediately flushed to disk.

careful write   An algorithm for updating a disk that prevents unexpected file system inconsistencies in the event of a system failure. A careful write file system serializes I/O requests and orders disk modifications so that any inconsistencies that do occur can be easily and fully repaired at a convenient time. Compare *lazy write.*

checkpoint record   A log file record NTFS writes periodically to help it determine what processing would be required to recover the volume if a crash occurred immediately. The log file service (LFS) stores the logical sequence number of the most recent checkpoint record in the log file's restart area so that NTFS can quickly find the log file's last checkpoint record when recovering from a crash. See also *log file, logical sequence numbers (LSNs), restart area, update record.*

cluster   The adjustable unit of disk allocation for the FAT file system and for NTFS. On the FAT file system, cluster size grows in proportion to the size of the disk. The NTFS cluster size is assignable but has a default size that is optimized for the disk's size.

cluster factor   The size of a cluster in NTFS. The cluster factor is the number of physical sectors (some power of 2) in the cluster and is generally expressed in bytes. See also *cluster*.

commit a transaction   To record in the log file the fact that a transaction is complete and has been recorded in the cache. See also *log file, transaction*.

compression engine   Code that implements a compression algorithm.

compression unit   A fixed-size quantity of disk data that is compressed, written, and read as a unit. The size of the compression unit in NTFS is 16 clusters.

dirty page table   A data structure NTFS maintains in memory to record which pages in the cache contain modifications to the file system structure that have not yet been written to disk. The dirty page table is used to implement file system recovery. See also *transaction table*.

duplex set   A variant of a mirror set in which the two volume partitions are on disks operated by different disk controllers—assuring data redundancy if a disk controller (rather than just a disk) fails. See also *mirror, mirror set*.

extent   See *run*.

FCB   file control block.

file control block (FCB)   An NTFS data structure used to find a file on disk, given a pointer to a file object. A file control block represents a single opened file and contains the file's file reference. See also *file reference, stream control block (SCB)*.

file namespace   The set of file names that are legal in an operating system environment. NTFS supports the file namespaces of MS-DOS–Windows, 32-bit Windows, OS/2 HPFS, and POSIX.

file record   The row in the master file table (MFT) that corresponds to a particular disk file. The file record is identified by its file reference. See also *file reference, master file table (MFT)*.

file reference   A 64-bit value, consisting of a sequence number and a file number, that NTFS uses to identify a file. The sequence number, used for internal consistency checks, is incremented each time an MFT file record position is reused. The file number corresponds to the position of the file's file record (or the file's base file record) in the master file table (MFT). See also *base file record, file record, master file table (MFT)*.

hard link count   A count of the number of POSIX file system directories that point to a file.

idempotent operation   An operation that has a neutral effect if it is executed more than once. NTFS redo and undo operations are designed to be idempotent.

index   A collection of file names selected for some file attribute and stored in a sorted order for quick access.

index buffer   A run of 2 KB or the cluster size (whichever is larger) that contains part of an index. Index buffers implement the b+ tree data structure used to sort index entries. See also *b+ tree*.

lazy write   An algorithm for updating a disk with the fastest possible throughput. Lazy write file systems write disk updates to a cache and flush the cache contents in an optimized way, often as a background activity. Lazy write file systems often risk data safety to achieve improved performance. Compare *careful write*.

lazy writer   A set of cache manager threads that call the virtual memory manager to flush cache contents to disk as a background activity. See also *cache manager*.

LCN   logical cluster number.

LFS   log file service.

log file   A file read and written by the log file service (LFS). The log file contains records of transaction suboperations NTFS writes to allow it to reconstruct an NTFS volume after a system failure. See also *log file service (LFS)*.

log file service (LFS)   A component of the Windows NT executive that provides services for logging disk modifications. NTFS calls the log file service to write a log file it uses to reconstruct an NTFS volume after a system failure. See also *log file*.

logging   A transaction-processing technique in which the suboperations of atomic transactions are recorded in a log file before they are written to disk. In the event of a system crash, fully logged transactions can be redone, and partially logged transactions can be undone, when the system comes back online. See also *log file, transaction*.

logging area   The region in the log file to which the log file service (LFS) writes NTFS records that are used to recover a volume in case of a system failure. The LFS makes the logging area appear infinite by reusing it circularly. See also *log file, log file service (LFS), restart area*.

logical cluster numbers (LCNs)   Instances resulting from the numbering, 0 to *n*, of the clusters on a volume from beginning to end. NTFS locates a cluster by multiplying its LCN by the volume's cluster factor, which yields the physical byte offset of the cluster. Compare *virtual cluster numbers (VCNs)*; see also *cluster, cluster factor*.

logical sequence numbers (LSNs)   Instances resulting from the numbering of records in the log file. The log file service (LFS) increases the values of LSNs as it writes records to the log file. The number of possible LSNs is virtually infinite. See also *log file*.

LSN   logical sequence number.

master file table (MFT)   The database that tracks the contents of an NTFS volume. The MFT is a table whose rows correspond to files on the volume and whose columns correspond to the attributes of each file.

metadata   The data and files NTFS uses to implement the file system structure.

MFT   master file table.

mirror   A disk volume used as a duplicate copy of an equal-sized or smaller volume on another disk in order to provide data redundancy. The Windows NT fault tolerant driver writes disk modifications to both the primary partition and its mirror partition.

mirror set   A set of two partitions on different disks, on one of which NTFS implements a mirror of the other. See also *mirror*.

mount   To prepare a volume for use. On NTFS, the mount process includes finding and opening file system files, copying some of their contents to memory, and executing the file system recovery procedure.

namespace   See *file namespace*.

nonresident attribute   A file attribute whose value is contained in one or more runs, or extents, outside the master file table (MFT) record and separate from the MFT. Compare *resident attribute*; see also *run*.

NT File System (NTFS)   The recoverable file system designed for use with the Windows NT operating system. NTFS uses database, transaction-processing, and object paradigms to provide data security, file system reliability, and advanced features not found in other mainstream file systems. See also *recoverable file system*.

NTFS   NT File System.

recoverable file system   A file system which ensures that if a power outage or other catastrophic system failure occurs, the file system won't be corrupted and no disk modifications will be left incomplete. The structure of the disk volume is restored to a consistent state when the system is rebooted.

redo information   Information in an update record that tells NTFS how to reapply a volume update, or transaction suboperation, during file system recovery. Compare *undo information*; see also *log file, update record*.

redo pass   The second of three scans NTFS makes through the log file during file system recovery. NTFS scans forward from the oldest logical sequence number (LSN) it found in the analysis pass and redoes the updates, or suboperations, of a transaction that was fully logged before the system failure but whose updates might not have been applied to the volume. Compare *analysis pass, undo pass*.

resident attribute   A file attribute whose value is wholly contained in the file's file record in the master file table (MFT). Compare *nonresident attribute*; see also *file record, master file table (MFT)*.

restart area   A region at the beginning of the log file in which the log file service (LFS) stores context information for itself and for NTFS. Information in the restart area allows NTFS to begin its volume recovery after a system failure. See also *log file, log file service (LFS), logging area*.

roll back   To undo a transaction whose logging in the log file was interrupted by a system failure. See also *transaction, transaction processing*.

run   Also called an *extent*. A contiguous disk allocation used to store part or all of a nonresident file attribute. See also *nonresident attribute*.

SCB   stream control block.

sector sparing   A feature of FtDisk, the Windows NT fault tolerant disk driver, in which an unreadable sector is dynamically replaced and its contents are restored. The data is either copied from a disk mirror or reconstructed from a stripe set with parity. Sector-sparing works only for SCSI-based hard disks that support it. See also *bad-cluster remapping.*

sparse files Files, often large, that contain only small amounts of nonzero data relative to their sizes.

stream A sequence of bytes.

stream control block (SCB) An NTFS data structure used to find a file on disk, given a pointer to a file object. A stream control block represents one attribute (stream) of an open file and points to the file control block for the file. See also *file control block (FCB).*

stripe A 64-KB area on equal-sized partitions on each of three or more disks. FtDisk, the Windows NT fault tolerant disk driver, writes data across the disks along the stripe, a technique that distributes data evenly among several disks, resulting in faster I/O performance. See also *stripe set, stripe set with parity.*

stripe set A series of same-size partitions, one per disk, that a file system accesses as a single logical volume. FtDisk, the Windows NT fault tolerant disk driver, implements stripe sets, writing data across the disks along 64-KB stripes. See also *stripe, stripe set with parity.*

stripe set with parity A fault tolerant variant of a stripe set in which the equivalent of one disk is used to record parity information for each stripe in the stripe set. If the data on one disk becomes inaccessible, FtDisk, the Windows NT fault tolerant disk driver, reconstructs the disk's contents by means of the parity information. See also *stripe set.*

transaction In NTFS, an atomic operation, one whose suboperations are treated as a single operation. The suboperations, or separate updates, of a transaction must all be completed successfully. If they aren't, those suboperations that were completed must be rolled back. See also *atomic transaction, commit a transaction, roll back.*

transaction processing A technique for modifying a database so that system failures do not compromise the correctness or integrity of the database. Every transaction is logged and then executed atomically. If a system failure occurs and interrupts the logging of the suboperations of the transaction, the log file is used to roll back the part of the transaction that was completed, returning the database to a previously known and consistent state. See also *log file, roll back, transaction.*

transaction table   A data structure NTFS maintains in memory to track transactions that have been started but that are not yet committed. The transaction table is used to implement file system recovery. See also *commit a transaction, dirty page table.*

undo information   Information in an update record that tells NTFS how to roll back a transaction whose updates, or suboperations, were not completely logged before a system failure. Compare *redo information*; see also *log file, roll back, update record.*

undo pass   The third of three scans NTFS makes through the log file during file system recovery. NTFS scans backward, rolling back the updates, or suboperations, of any transaction that wasn't fully logged, or committed, when the system failed. Compare *analysis pass, redo pass.*

update record   A log file record NTFS writes to register a volume update, or transaction suboperation, before writing the change to the volume. An update record contains redo and undo information for the volume update. See also *checkpoint record, redo information, undo information.*

VCN   virtual cluster number.

virtual cluster numbers (VCNs)   Instances resulting from the numbering, 0 to *m*, of the clusters containing the nonresident attributes of a file. NTFS maps a file's VCNs to LCNs in order to find the file's clusters on the disk. Compare *logical cluster numbers (LCNs)*; see also *cluster, nonresident attribute.*

virtual memory manager   The component of the Windows NT executive that implements virtual memory.

volume   A logical partition on a disk, created when the disk is formatted for a particular file system. NTFS volumes can span multiple disks. See also *volume set.*

volume file   The NTFS file that contains the volume's name, the version of NTFS for which the volume is formatted, and a "dirty bit" that, when set, signifies that a disk corruption has occurred which must be repaired by the Chkdsk utility.

volume set   A series of free areas (as many as 32) on one or more disks that NTFS formats and accesses as a single volume. See also *volume.*

write-ahead logging   A logging technique in which log file records are guaranteed to be flushed to disk before any of the corresponding volume updates are written to disk. See also *log file, logging, update record.*

BIBLIOGRAPHY

Ayre, Rick, and Robin Raskin. "Windows NT: See How It Runs." *PC Magazine* 12, no. 16 (September 28, 1993): 211–31.

Custer, Helen. *Inside Windows NT.* Redmond, Wash.: Microsoft Press, 1993.

Duncan, Ray. "Design Goals and Implementation of the New High Performance File System." *Microsoft Systems Journal* (September 1989): 1–13.

Duncan, Ray. *Advanced MS-DOS Programming,* 2d ed. Redmond, Wash.: Microsoft Press, 1988. The "Disk Internals" chapter of this now-classic volume contains a discussion of the FAT file system.

Karth, H. F., and A. Silberschatz. *Database System Concepts,* 2d ed. New York: McGraw Hill, 1991.

Patterson, A., Garth Gibson, and Randy H. Katz. "A Case for Redundant Arrays of Inexpensive Disks, or RAID." Univ. of California at Berkeley, report no. UCB/CSD 87/391, December 1987.

Silberschatz, Abraham, and Peter Galvin. *Operating System Concepts,* 4th ed. Reading, Mass.: Addison-Wesley, 1994.

Udell, Jon. "Is There a Better Windows 3.1 Than Windows 3.1?" *Byte* 18, no. 12 (November 1993): 85–96.

The Unicode Consortium. *The Unicode Standard: World-Wide Character Encoding,* version 1.0, 2 vols. Reading, Mass.: Addison-Wesley, 1991–92. The prepublication edition of Unicode version 1.1 (which requires version 1.0) is also available as "Unicode Technical Report no. 4," from the Unicode Consortium (415-961-4189). The report is also available on Internet at unicode-inc@unicode.org). The prepublication edition is also available on the Microsoft Developer's Network compact discs.

INDEX

Page numbers in italics refer to figures.

Special Characters

: (colon), as separator, 8
$ (dollar sign), for attributes, 22
. (periods), in names, 9

A

aliases, file name, 70–71, *72*
allocation, file. *See* file system; MFT (master file table)
analysis pass in recovery operation, 45, *45,* 75
Andrew, Brian, 1n, 12
APIs (application programming interfaces), 7, 75
Apple Macintosh data and resources, NTFS data streams for, 8
application programming interfaces. *See* APIs (application programming interfaces)
atomic transaction, 14–15, 75
attribute list attribute, 23, 28
attributes
  definition tables for, 32, 75
  identifying, 22
  indexing, 9
  in the master file table (MFT), 15–16, *16*
  order of, 24
  resident and nonresident, 24–26, *25, 26*
  system-defined, 23
  user-defined, *16,* 16n
authorization, security descriptor for, 5, *15, 16,* 23

B

b+ tree structure, 16, 28–29, 75
bad clusters
  file of, 32, 75

bad clusters, *continued*
  recovering, 55–59
  remapping, 9, 75
bad-sector errors, spare sectors for, 54–55
base file record, 21, 75
batching log records, 36
Bernoulli disks, 10
bitmap attribute
  described, 23
  in MFT file records, 26, *26*
  for VCNs, 29
bitmap file
  allocation data in, *31,* 31
  defined, 76
  as a volume file, 50
boot file
  defined, 76
  as MFT file record, 21
  in mounting, 30
  overview, *31,* 31
bootstrap code, 30–31
buffer. *See also* cache
  decompressed data, 66
  index, 26, 28–29

C

cache. *See also* buffer
  decompressed data, 66
  flushing, 36–37, 76
  lazy write file systems and, 35–36
  in recoverable file systems, 37
  write-through, 37, 76
cache manager
  defined, 76
  for log files, 38, *38,* 39–40, 43
  overview, 12–13, *13*
cache misses, 13, 65n
careful write file systems, 34–35, 76
case-sensitive names, 9
checkpoint record, 42–43, *43,* 76
Chkdsk utility
  for bad sectors, 33n, 55, 57, 58
  HPFS, 36
cluster
  bad-cluster recovery, 55–59

Helen Custer

Helen Custer is the author of *Inside Windows NT* and of numerous articles on operating systems and language topics. A member of the Windows NT development team for five years, she is responsible for chronicling the architecture and design of the operating system.

COVER DESIGNER
Rebecca Geisler-Johnson

INTERIOR GRAPHIC DESIGNER
Kim Eggleston

INTERIOR GRAPHIC ARTIST
David Holter

PRINCIPAL TYPOGRAPHER
Ruth Pettis

PRINCIPAL EDITORIAL COMPOSITOR
Barb Runyan

PRINCIPAL PROOFREADER/COPY EDITOR
Alice Copp Smith

INDEXER
Ted Laux

The manuscript for this book was prepared and submitted to Microsoft Press in electronic form. Text files were prepared using Microsoft Word 2.0 for Windows. Pages were composed by Microsoft Press using Aldus PageMaker 5.0 for Windows, with text in New Baskerville and display type in Helvetica Bold. Composed pages were delivered to the printer as electronic prepress files.

Microsoft® Windows NT™ Resource Kit

Microsoft Corporation

This exclusive three-volume Microsoft collection is a comprehensive source of technical information and tools necessary to support Windows NT installations. The *Microsoft Windows NT Resource Kit* includes *Windows NT Resource Guide* (with four 3.5-inch disks), *Windows NT Messages* (with three 3.5-inch disks), and *Optimizing Windows NT* (with one 3.5-inch disk). The three volumes are also available separately.

BONUS! The three-volume set also includes a CD-ROM containing all the disk-based utilities PLUS tools and utilities for RISC-based computers.

Three-volume set boxed with eight 3.5-inch disks and one CD-ROM
$109.95 ($148.95 Canada)   ISBN 1-55615-602-2

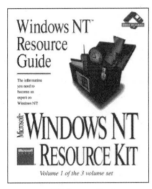

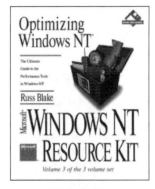

Volume 1:
Windows NT Resource Guide

This complete technical guide to Windows NT features information about installing, configuring, customizing, and troubleshooting Windows NT. It also includes information on applications compatibility and migration from Windows 3.1, MS-DOS, OS/2, and LAN Manager, and using database services with Windows NT. The four disks include more than 50 tools, utilities, and value-added software, including tools to manage users and groups of servers, a computer profile setup to easily set up large groups of workstations, an adapter card Help file, an online registry Help file, and utilities for the POSIX subsystem.

1024 pages, with four 3.5-inch disks
$49.95 ($67.95 Canada)
ISBN 1-55615-598-0

Volume 2:
Windows NT Messages

An alphabetic reference and online database that provides in-depth, accessible information about Windows NT and Windows NT Advanced Server error and system-information messages. Also includes detailed discussions about Windows NT executive messages and an extensive glossary of common message terms and user actions. The messages have been loaded into a Microsoft Access database with a simple user interface, which enables the user to search the database, add personal notes under a message, back up the database, and print a selected group of messages. The three disks contain a runtime version of Microsoft Access and the Messages database.

624 pages with three 3.5-inch disks
$39.95 ($53.95 Canada)
ISBN 1-55615-600-6

Volume 3:
Optimizing Windows NT

The one resource that provides all the information needed to maximize the capacity and speed of Windows NT, including information on bottleneck detection and capacity planning for the desktop and network. Also includes information on designing and tuning your Windows NT applications for high performance. Included with the book is one disk full of software accessories and utilities for performance monitoring, troubleshooting, fine-tuning, and optimizing PC performance.

608 pages with one 3.5-inch disk
$34.95 ($46.95 Canada)
ISBN 1-55615-619-7

*Microsoft*Press

Microsoft Press® books are available wherever quality books are sold and through CompuServe's Electronic Mall—GO MSP.
Call 1-800-MSPRESS for direct ordering information or for placing credit card orders.*
Please refer to BBK when placing your order. Prices subject to change.

*In Canada, contact Macmillan Canada, Attn: Microsoft Press Dept., 164 Commander Blvd., Agincourt, Ontario, Canada M1S 3C7, or call 1-800-667-1115.
Outside the U.S. and Canada, write to International Coordinator, Microsoft Press, One Microsoft Way, Redmond WA 98052-6399.

Information from the Source

Microsoft® Windows NT™ Step by Step

Catapult, Inc.

MICROSOFT WINDOWS NT STEP BY STEP provides easy-to-use, self-paced training for using Windows NT. Whether you are a new user or are upgrading from Windows 3.1, this training package—complete with timesaving practice files on disk—can teach you exactly what you need to know and when you need to know it. In addition to mastering the basics of Windows NT, you'll quickly learn how to use Mail, Schedule+, and Windows NT-based applications. If you're too busy to attend class, or if classroom training doesn't make sense for you or your office, you can train yourself with this *Step by Step* book from Microsoft Press.

360 pages, softcover with one 3.5-inch disk
$29.95 ($39.95 Canada) ISBN 1-55615-573-5

Running Windows NT™

Craig Stinson with Mike Blaszczak, Bruce McKinney, and JoAnne Woodcock

Get up and running fast with Windows NT with this outstanding guide from *PC Magazine* contributing editor Craig Stinson. Full of examples, illustrations, tips, and strategies, RUNNING WINDOWS NT is your comprehensive guide to setting up, using, and optimizing this powerful software. It includes expert information and advice on Windows NT basics, networking, optimization, and security and administration. Plus a table of contents for each section and chapter and an expanded, cross-referenced index with more than 1200 entries help make finding answers easier. And when you're up and running and ready to go beyond the basics, you'll find advanced information and undocumented tips, strategies, and solutions.

848 pages $27.95 ($37.95 Canada) ISBN 1-55615-572-7

Inside Windows NT™

Helen Custer
Foreword by David N. Cutler

INSIDE WINDOWS NT provides an accessible, inside look at the design of this revolutionary operating system. Written by a member of the Windows NT team during the system's development, this book reads like a wide-ranging, in-depth discussion with the Windows NT developers. The author begins with a description of the Windows NT operating system and a discussion of the design goals, providing an overview of Windows NT and the architectural model on which it is based, and moves on to more technical topics: the NT kernel, virtual memory manager, object management, client-server protected subsystems, processes and threads, future directions, and much more.

416 pages, softcover $24.95 ($32.95 Canada) ISBN 1-55615-481-X

*Microsoft*Press

Microsoft Press books are available wherever quality books are sold and through CompuServe's Electronic Mall—GO MSP.
Call 1-800-MSPRESS for direct ordering information or for placing credit card orders.*
Please refer to BBK when placing your order. Prices subject to change.
*In Canada, contact Macmillan Canada, Attn: Microsoft Press Dept., 164 Commander Blvd., Agincourt, Ontario, Canada M1S 3C7, or call 1-800-667-1115.
Outside the U.S. and Canada, write to International Coordinator, Microsoft Press, One Microsoft Way, Redmond WA 98052-6399.